Fusion Management

Harnessing the Power of Six Sigma,
Lean, ISO 9001:2000, Malcolm
Baldrige, TQM and Other
Quality Breakthroughs
of the Past Century

Dr. Stanley A. Marash
with Paul Berman and Michael Flynn

QSU
Publishing Company

This publication is designed to provide accurate and authoritative information in regard to the subject matter covered. It is sold with the understanding that neither the author nor the publisher is engaged in rendering legal, accounting or other professional service. If legal advice or other expert assistance is required, the services of a competent professional person should be sought.

Printed in the United States of America. The publisher of this book was Paul Scicchitano. It was set in Times New Roman and Palatino by Suzanne E. Leonard.

For more information, contact QSU Publishing Company, 3975 University Drive, Suite 230, Fairfax, Virginia 22030 USA or online at www.qsuonline.com.

Dedication

To my mother Esther, who always tells me I can do anything I want to, and my wife Muriel, who prods me to stretch even more.

Acknowledgments

My thanks to my executive assistant, Marianne Thomas, who took us through many revisions of this material, and to Roni Salkin, director of publications, who edited the material.

Table of Contents

Introduction

Everything we need to know about quality was published by 1931. Yet today, in the 21st century, we are still struggling with what it all means. We have all heard someone say, "If it weren't for our customers…" But we realize that if it weren't for our customers, we wouldn't have jobs.

A common wall plaque says:

The past is history.

The future is a mystery.

The present is a gift.

Most of us don't realize how much of a gift the present is. We are writing this book during the aftermath of the destruction by terrorists of the World Trade Center in New York City, and we are very much aware of the present and concerned about the future.

In writing this book, we chose to dwell on the past century to help us understand the present and, hopefully, influence the future. The past, we believe, contains valuable insights into the quality revolution that followed the technological advances of the past century. We have tried to examine what has worked, and what hasn't; what was properly deployed, and what wasn't; what was assimilated, and what was discarded. The future should be less of a mystery if we open our eyes and not allow ourselves to make the same mistakes over and over.

Today, disciplines like Six Sigma and Lean Enterprise are producing widely heralded results in all types of industries. But previous management approaches have also produced excellent results, only to fall into disuse and disappear. In this book we examine some of these trends to try to learn why they eventually failed.

We have tried to comprehend what has gone before at the strategic level, the tactical level and the operational level. Our focus is on fusing the products of these three levels such that the synergies provide us with business results that enable order-of-magnitude improvements.

We have used this approach to construct a model for Fusion Management that is robust enough to fit enterprises of all sizes (small, medium, large) and all areas of application (services, research and development, manufacturing, education, health care, government).

We hope this book provides you with some insights as to why we do things the way we do them, and how we can build on the things we are doing well to make our organization substantially better.

1

Management by Fad
(or *Confusion* Management)

INTRODUCTION: MANAGEMENT FADS AND WHY THEY FAIL

Several years ago I was invited by the European Organization for Quality (EOQ) and the United Kingdom's Institute of Quality Assurance (IQA) to participate in the EOQ's forum, "Quality in Integrated Management." At this conference, I was asked to synthesize the presentations and to offer insights on the future of quality approaches and philosophy over the next five or more years. The four topics selected were:

- ❖ Standards approach to management.
- ❖ Breakthrough management.
- ❖ Business excellence awards.
- ❖ Integrated management.

About five years have passed since that conference, and these four topics are clearly still central to management discussions in the new millennium.

After reading the papers that had been provided for my review, I began to think about the various quality-related programs I had been exposed to since 1960, when I began my career as a quality professional. Doodling on a pad, I quickly listed 32 programs that had come and, for the most part, gone — an average of almost one per year. These are listed in Figure 1-1.

Most organizations have tried at least a few of these programs, sometimes more than one at a time. Many of them are so taken with *management by imi-*

tation that they introduce new programs at an average rate of one every three years, almost always capturing only the superficial aspects of the program. The employees of such organizations learn to pay lip service to each new management fad without letting it interfere with "real work," knowing full well that it will soon go away. It was in response to this approach that I coined the term *programme du jour* — program of the day.

As I studied the list, I began to look for trends or patterns. Why had some companies succeeded while others failed? And why had some succeeded initially only to fail later? The circumstances of individual companies differed — in their culture, history, personalities — but this is what a statistician would call "noise." Could there be a signal underneath the noise? The more I studied the list and considered the history of each movement, the more I realized that there are, indeed, perpetually recurring causes of failure.

FIGURE 1-1 PROGRAMMES DU JOUR

Benchmarking	Process Management
Breakthrough Management	Profit Improvement
Business Excellence Awards	Program Management
Business Partnerships	Quality Circles
Companywide Quality Control	Reengineering
Concurrent Engineering	Reinventing Government
Continuous Quality Improvement	Rightsizing
Cost Reduction	Statistical Process Control
Downsizing	Strategic Planning
Holistic Management	Total Quality Control
Integrated Management	Total Quality Management
Just-In-Time	Value Analysis
Management by Objectives	Value Engineering
Managerial Breakthrough	Vendor (Supplier) Partnership
One-Minute Management	Voice of the Customer
Outsourcing	Zero Defects

Lack of Executive Leadership — Management fails to demonstrate its commitment *by deeds* to the process it is launching. Indeed, many such programs are initiated and led by mid-level managers with little, if any, involvement by executives. Even when executives become involved, their efforts are seldom substantive. The organizations that are successful over the long term, regardless of the program implemented, invariably feature the personal leadership of executive teams.

Failure To Deploy — Management fails to support the program beyond the initial training or to deploy the program beyond the pilot department or group. After an initial round of improvement is achieved, no mechanism is established to keep the process going. Program activities are perceived as "homework," rather than "real work," and because many projects concentrate on "low-hanging fruit," the program stalls once its larger and less tractable problems are encountered. Other times, different groups within an organization adopt different programs — and then spend valuable time and resources hurling buzzwords at each other rather than searching for common ground. Successful organizations, on the other hand, synthesize their own programs from many sources, actively engage all groups at all levels and develop permanent structures to identify and resolve problems.

Seeking Shortcuts — Management adopts the superficial aspects of a program, hoping by name-magic to imitate the successes of the pioneer organizations. Yet, the pioneers usually developed well thought-out processes involving many contributing elements. Organizations that adopt some elements and ignore others fail to attain the synergy that the pioneers achieved and later proclaim: "We tried X program and it didn't work." In some cases, management does nothing more than attach a new, trendy label to an old way of doing business.

Inadequate Measurement — Management does not measure success properly. These organizations typically don't lack measurements — indeed, they are often guilty of *overmeasuring*. The problem with these organizations is that their measurements are detached from business results. Projects concentrate on making internal processes more efficient while overlooking customer satisfaction, because the former is easier to measure than the latter. Successful organizations, on the other hand, focus on the long term as well as the short term and on external as well as internal issues and tie their measurements to validated business results.

A common pattern emerges. A few pioneer companies adopt or develop a program and achieve great initial success. The business press takes notice and other companies seek to emulate the pioneers. But as the idea spreads, it becomes diluted. Senior management tries to adopt the model without ever really comprehending what is required to make the program successful. These followers want the results but are unwilling to put in the same effort as the pioneers. They fail to measure their results and they lack clear, focused goals. It is almost as if ideas have a half-life, like fissionable materials, losing substance as they pass from organization to organization.

What is needed is fusion, not fission.

In *fission*, a process of decay causes material to split apart, creating a great deal of heat and, over time, lead. In *fusion*, simpler elements combine to form more complex elements, which take on features and qualities that the constituent ingredients did not possess. Hence, we call our concept "Fusion Management."

LESSONS FROM THE PAST AND WHAT THEY TEACH

For the past half-century, organizations have been struggling to develop and implement good management practices to help them become more successful and profitable. Let's take a look at a few of these programs and try to learn from their shortcomings.

Statistical Quality Control (SQC) — During the 1920s and 1930s, quality practitioners noted that industrial processes behaved statistically; that is, all data are fuzzy and temporary. Data are "fuzzy" because no measurement is perfectly precise and all samples are estimates. They are "temporary" because the processes from which they originate are dynamic and do not consist, as A. C. Rosander once commented, of "a fixed number of colored balls in an urn." To compensate for this inherent fuzziness, practitioners invented two tools, acceptance sampling and the so-called control chart. Acceptance sampling, developed by Harold Dodge and Harry Romig in the 1920s, took sampling variation into account when judging whether a lot contained more than a specified number of defectives. The basic idea was simple: All sampling, whether statistically based or not, may inadvertently reject lots that are acceptable or, conversely, accept lots that are not. Statistical methods quantify the risks of committing these two types of errors (also known as "alpha risk" and "beta risk," respectively). Hence, they allow us to choose economic sampling sizes to provide reasonable protection against rejecting good product or accepting bad product.

The stumbling block was the concept of "acceptable quality level" (AQL) — the level of defective material that is more economical to deal with in the process phase than to completely sort out and rectify (repair or reject) prior to use. If a lot exceeds the AQL, it is cheaper to sort it out. If a lot is below this level, it is cheaper to accept it and find the defects in subsequent operations.

But while the AQL was solely intended to help management decide whether defectives should be handled before or after a gate point in a process, it was used in practice to decide how many defectives per lot would be considered "okay." One vice president even said (with a smile on his face) that using AQLs meant that his customers could no longer complain if he sent them a few defectives.

Acceptance sampling was superseded, starting in the 1940s, by the concept of statistical control, originally developed in the 1920s by Walter Shewhart. In a statistically controlled process essentially all lots are of the same quality. Acceptance sampling becomes unnecessary since the organization *knows* on which side of the divide the lots are and all components of a lot are either used as-is with defects corrected *en passant*, or sorted and rectified prior to use. Only when the process' output is uncertain do individual lots need particular attention, and Shewhart's control charts signal when that happens so the causes can be found and corrected. For example, a check clearinghouse learns that an increase in the number of check processing errors is the result of a change in procedure; a pharmaceutical packaging operation discovers that a shift in the print registration is the result of the replacement of the ruler used to measure it.

Shewhart's chart was, and is, an extremely powerful diagnostic tool, and statistical thinking is indeed much more precise than anecdotal thinking. However, diagnostics no more lead to organizational excellence than a thermometer cures disease. SQC may be an essential measurement aid, but it is no more than that.

Moreover, a process "in control" will produce a predictable number of defects or errors. However, an operation can be predictably poor. Misapplications of SQC led many companies to stabilize their defect levels and then accept the remaining defectives as "inevitable." Top practitioners knew better. W. Edwards Deming once said that statistical control means the process is "doing the best it can," but that being the case, "perhaps we should take some dynamite and alter the process." This vital point was lost on many. By the time most statistical methods reached the floor, they had been reduced to mechanical and formulaic procedures applied without real understanding.

SQC had a second life in the 1950s as Statistical Process Control (SPC) with a welcome emphasis on process thinking; in practice, it suffered from the same misunderstandings as its earlier incarnation. SPC was widely perceived as "something the operator does" or as "measuring and plotting" rather than as a wider body of knowledge focused on improvement and control. I can count more than 50 plants that I visited over the years, where each had literally hundreds of control charts, but not a single one being used to diagnose and improve processes. The charts were kept because certain customers required it. In one Pennsylvania bottling plant a statistician told me that he had searched long and hard for dozens of characteristics that were *naturally in control* because a large customer had arbitrarily demanded "80 percent of charts submitted each month be in a state of control." A company manager in a Michigan car manufacturing plant proudly led me into a room that was literally wallpapered with control charts — all of them badly out of control, with no effort being made to discover the assignable causes. But that didn't matter to the manager who was giving me the tour because, as far as he was concerned, the company *had* SPC. In each of these cases companies made the mistake of forgetting that SPC is something you *do*, not something you *have*. In fact, I often counsel clients to drive their processes *out of control* in a *positive direction* — towards improvement.

Management by Objectives (MBO) — MBO, which took the corporate world by storm in the 1960s, was based on a simple and apparently inarguable idea. Set measurable, quantifiable "stretch" goals and evaluate yourself against them. Executive management would set top-level goals for the organization. Based on these, middle managers would set their own business unit, divisional and departmental goals and so on down the chain. Since all objectives would be tied to the overall goals, the efforts of all departments would be coordinated. Because the objectives were to be measurable, managers would know where they stood, and performance evaluations would be clear-cut. And finally, since managers were to choose "stretch" goals, the organization would improve its performance.

So much for theory. The reality was that those who diligently followed the model achieved admirable results, but they were followed by those who wanted to "have MBO" rather than to manage their objectives. Executives would set some vague goal — "reduce waste by five percent" was a popular one — and promulgate it via the internal memo. When it reached the supervisory level, the goal was still "reduce waste by five percent," the middle levels having done nothing to clarify or particularize the objective through analysis or prioritization. In some cases, managers formed goals by compiling their supervisor's goals. That is, the objectives cascaded *up* the organization, resulting in chaos rather than an increased level of efficiency. In many cases a department would achieve its "goals" simply by pushing its work off onto others and then publicizing its own "increased efficiency."

Managers very quickly learned to "game the system" and proposed so-called *stretch* goals that were already well in hand but had not yet been recognized by higher management. For example, in 1962 I met the vice president of human resources for an appliance manufacturer in Ohio who went as far as to define one of his stretch goals as "*to develop a health and safety course and train all employees by the end of next year*," when the course had already been created and plans for presenting it were already in place. It is easy to hit the target when you draw the bull's eye around the arrow!

In another case a Pittsburgh steel mill turning out 100,000 tons of material set a goal of 120,000 tons for the following year. The next year, when production had reached only 108,000 tons, the mill reported achieving 90 percent of its goal!

I have even encountered cases where setting objectives has hurt a company's productivity. In the late 1960s, while evaluating the productivity of a large New York financial clearinghouse, I met an administrative supervisor who was faced with the usual "reduce waste by five percent" goal — in this case, it was in the form of incorrectly processed documents. The supervisor confided that he had two ideas, either one of which would save the five percent. But he planned to implement only one of the two, saving the other for next year's MBO. In other words, MBO actually held him back!

Ultimately, the misapplication of MBO resulted in companies vigorously pursuing objectives that kept them standing still, or even falling behind.

Karl Albrecht, in *Successful Management by Objectives*, wrote in 1978: "[MBO] is not a system. It is not a method. It is not a procedure. It is a concept. It is a philosophy. It is a basic mentality which the high performance manager brings to the job of managing." This, of course, is its fundamental weakness. A "mentality" is a frame of mind, not a plan of action. Therefore, its success depends on conversion rather than on effort.

There is nothing wrong with MBO. Managers really should set measurable stretch goals in coordination with overall organizational goals. But *pursued by itself* it will seldom achieve its promise. As Albrecht also wrote, "Many of these [MBO] efforts have led to frustration, disappointment and disillusionment. This has given the term "Management by Objectives" a spotty reputation among practical-minded business managers."

Zero Defects (ZD) — The Zero Defects concept was developed by defense contractor Martin Marietta and popularized by Philip B. Crosby in the 1970s. Crosby and other ZD advocates saw the flaw in the AQL concept (and of being "in control" at an average level of defectives). He parodied the attitude in an address to the Rocky Mountain Quality Conference in which he spoke of the Two Defects Program. Every unit produced would have to have two defects. That was the goal. If a unit had only one defect, it would have to be tracked down and a second defect added. People took notes; this worried him.

The ZD concept is very simple. How many errors do you *want* to give your customer? This is best understood by asking how many defects you want to purchase from your supplier. Most people have no problem insisting on ZD when it comes to their own paychecks.

The use of sampling techniques that focused on achieving an acceptable quality level (AQL) created a mind-set that a certain level of defects was acceptable. ZD tried to combat this notion. If we convinced everybody that they should not have errors in their own activities — that they should not tolerate defects — we could in fact achieve zero defects, or something very close to that.

Typically, companies embarking on ZD programs sponsored kick-off events in which employees would sign pledge cards committing themselves to the goal of achieving zero defects. "ZD Day" might include a marching band, gifts and tokens to be distributed.

Unfortunately, the premise on which this effort was established was flawed. It assumed that defects resulted from operator error. However, most errors or defects — some scholars put the figure as high as 90 percent — are the result of the system in which people work. That is, they are "management controllable" rather than "operator controllable." Regardless of their dedication or diligence workers are limited by their equipment, their materials, the procedures they must follow and so forth. Joseph M. Juran, for example, analyzed the typographical errors made by linotype operators. The basic cause was poor equipment maintenance; management had been squeezing the budget for years. Consequently, the machines themselves made mistakes and the operators, knowing that their work would have to be hand-corrected anyway, had little motivation to correct their own typos.

Around 1964, when I was working for RCA as a quality manager, I was called into the general manager's office. He told me that all of the company's operations that were contracting to the Department of Defense were going to adopt a Zero Defects program. Having read quite a bit about the effort, I suggested a list of things that we needed to do before we had a kick-off meeting. The general manager responded, "Don't worry, corporate has everything in hand. Just call the Corporate Zero Defects Office and they will supply you with pledge cards, gifts and suggested programming for the kick-off day event." Realizing that this program had about zero probability of success, I managed to have someone else arrange it. The kick-off session was a major success. There was a great deal of excitement. Employees were pleased that there was an error identification card that they could use to identify potential sources of defects. They took the campaign seriously and filled out the forms. In fact, in a very short period of time, the 2,000 employees of our division had submitted over 3,000 error identification cards. Management had promised that they would respond to each card and provide follow-up. However, it was immediately obvious that a one-person industrial engineering department could not possibly keep up with the workload. The program faded away in less than six months due to a lack of foresight and commitment on the part of management.

Insofar as they set a goal of continual improvement toward zero, ZD practitioners had the right idea. But this was also its fundamental weakness. ZD programs pointed out the direction the organization needed to go, but they did not show how to get there. Enthusiasm and motivation are well and good, but desire is not a substitute for skill. It's one thing to *want* to reduce errors, but quite another thing to *achieve* a reduction in errors. ZD is like picking the top of Mount Everest as your travel destination without having a plan, budget and resources for getting there.

Quality Circles — During the late 1970s and early 1980s, the Japanese economy was very stong and many managers wanted to know "how the Japanese did it." The answer is complex, but a common feature of Japanese companies was the Quality Control (QC) circle, which later became very popular in the West.

QC circles (called quality circles in the West) were made up of workers trained in basic problem-solving and statistical tools who selected and implemented improvement projects within their work groups. Unfortunately, the results in Western companies did not meet the expectations of management. Although a small percentage of projects achieved substantial results, most did not. Moreover, the great majority of QC achievements were "feel good" results, such as beautifying the workplace. In other cases, QC project solutions were never even deployed. The US version of quality circles was doomed from the start.

The fundamental concept was sound. The people doing the work often have insights and creative ideas for resolving their problems. But this was also the fundamental flaw, because the problems they addressed and their ideas for handling them necessarily had a limited horizon. A QC circle, for example, might come up with brilliant ideas on how to assemble an Edsel more efficiently, but it will never realize that Edsels are not what they should be assembling. That is, both the problems chosen and the solutions implemented tend to be local.

Dr. Juran pointed out that in any organization there are a few problems that are individually of great magnitude and a host of smaller problems that individually do not have as great an impact. He called this the *Pareto Principle*, after the Italian economist Vilfredo Pareto, and used it to describe a class of statistical distributions sometimes called rank-size laws. The first group, which he called *the vital few*, tends to be management controllable and typically accounts for 80 to 90 percent of total losses. The remainder, *the useful many*, is too small to merit the attention of managers, engineers and other specialists, but may be addressed fruitfully by the workforce using QC circles. The Japanese used this approach, but they did not neglect the vital few. In fact, the Japanese quality revolution was 10 years old before the first QC circle arose in the West. Westerners who adopted QC circles often forgot (or did not know) that they were only part of what the Japanese were doing.

Western managers also failed to understand that consensus decision making in Japan was built around a homogeneous society and a distinct type of corporate culture, as William Ouchi pointed out in his 1981 book, *Theory Z.*

Had management understood its own role — that they were responsible for defining vision and allocating resources — they could have applied the same kinds of successful management practices to quality circles as they were using for other efforts. Such practices might have included, for example, adapting the concept to suit their particular corporate cultures, planning how to implement it, clearly delegating responsibility and authority for each project, setting measurable and *meaningful* goals, evaluating results and recognizing and rewarding successful projects — all in conjunction with a broader effort that would include an attack on the vital few.

Deep down, many managers did not believe in the distinction between management-controllable and operator-controllable problems. They suspected that the work force was the source of all errors, so it made sense that workers should get together in their circles to fix them. Hence, managers had unrealistic expectations of the improvements that could be achieved by QC circles. So when results failed to measure up to expectations, management discarded the program rather than their expectations. Such misunderstandings led management to abandon a potentially useful source of business process improvements.

Total Quality Management (TQM) — Perhaps no initiative was more widely tried and more widely misunderstood than Total Quality Management. The basic idea is very simple: "qualities" (the features of a product or service) are "managed" by the total effort of the organization. Armand Feigenbaum first put forward this idea in 1961 to combat the notion that only the operating departments were responsible for the qualities of the output. Rather, every function within the organization contributes to quality and hence to customer satisfaction. For example, the marketing function discovers which functional features the customer would like and design/planning determines the technical features that the product must have to satisfy those functional needs.

Each activity within an organization produces a "product," which it passes on to other activities. Maintenance produces "repairs." Quality control produces "inspection data." Payroll produces "paychecks." Each product has features (qualities) that make it fit for use by those downstream (repairs, for example, must be timely and effective). It is therefore the responsibility of each individual in the organization to assure the quality of the aspects of his or her own output that contribute to the final output of the organization. Stated in this fashion, the proposition seems self-evident. Yet, the execution of TQM left a great deal to be desired.

Nothing in TQM prevented goal setting, but goals were not an inherent component of TQM programs. Consequently, organizations applied the concept only as a "good thing to do" without considering exactly what they planned to do with it.

In some companies, TQM was little more than QC circles on a larger scale. Some employees reported that their "TQM training" consisted of nothing more than behavioral skills and teamwork. While such training is important and valuable, it does not address the whole of TQM. In too many cases not only was TQM not "total," but it failed to address "quality" and "management." Lacking a quantifiable direction (such as "zero defects" or "six sigma quality") and leadership commitment, these programs lost momentum and soon petered out.

Use of Standards as Management Models — Today's "standards" approach to management is one of the more widespread management approaches, and whole industries have moved to adopt it. In this paradigm the management system is designed around compliance with, or registration to, one or more consensus or regulatory standards, for example:

- ❖ ISO 9001 for quality management.
- ❖ ISO 14001 for environmental management.
- ❖ CE (Conformite Europeene) marking for certain European Union regulated products.
- ❖ US Code of Federal Regulations — e.g., 21 CFR 820 — Good Manufacturing Practice for Medical Devices (Quality System Requirements).

These system models are frequently augmented by sector-specific standards, such as:

- ❖ QS-9000 and ISO/TS 16949 for the automotive industry.
- ❖ TL 9000 for telecommunications.
- ❖ AS9100 for aerospace.

In most of these models an independent third-party auditing firm, called a *registrar*, audits an organization's management system to verify compliance with the applicable standard or standards. In some cases there is an option for self-declaration of compliance.

At one time there were a host of different standards — military, nuclear, NASA, FDA. Each of the Big Three automakers had its own system. Depending on its line of business, an organization might find itself audited by several customers and agencies, each using a standard with slightly different requirements. This practice often required maintaining duplicate and parallel procedures. So the idea of a single standard audited by a third party was very attractive. It saved the second party (the customer) from the cost of performing multiple audits on its suppliers; and it saved the first party (the supplier) from the hassle of multiple audits by several customers.

Unfortunately, many consultants and registrars have diminished the value of this approach. They tell companies to "get registered now, you can always improve later." This philosophy is often expressed by statements such as "just document what you do and do what you document, and you will get registered and save money."

However, hanging a plaque in the lobby does not save money nor does it improve quality. *The real savings come not from getting registered but from what a company does on the way to registration.*

Most management systems include a significant number of non-value-added activities. These accumulate over time, like barnacles on a ship — redundant forms, multiple signature requirements, extra inspections and so forth. If an organization merely "documents what it does," it will institutionalize its wasteful practices, and thus perpetuate the waste. Furthermore, in the process of documenting its practices, auditing them and maintaining additional records as proof of performing them, the organization incurs additional costs. Thus, the net result is higher not lower costs. To realize savings the processes must usually be reengineered (in the genuine meaning of the much-abused term) *before* they are documented and implemented. That is, the savings come from the work that is done leading up to registration, not from the registration itself.

While most organizations will benefit from adhering to a well-planned management system, the concept is inherently static and bureaucratic. ISO 9000 and related management system approaches emphasize standards, records, audits and corrective action. This emphasis has led to widespread acceptance — organizations use recognizable management practices and no one has to learn anything esoteric. However, it is also a fundamental flaw. It has been said that you can get registered for making concrete life vests, provided you follow your procedures for making them. ISO 9001 requires organizations to learn the requirements of their customers and it is difficult to imagine much customer demand for concrete life vests. But the overall tenor of the remark is not mistaken. Neither standards compliance nor the registration process directly addresses excellent results.

Because of this, the most recent revision, ISO 9001:2000, explicitly specifies continual improvement as a requirement for maintaining conformance. However, the standard does not (and should not) prescribe a particular manner of achieving improvement, so it is clear that standards-based systems *by themselves* cannot be entirely effective. It remains to be seen if third-party auditors can adequately assess whether continual improvement has been built into an organization's processes.

JIT and Reengineering — Other examples of shortcut thinking arose with the "Just-In-Time (JIT)" and "reengineering" crazes of the 1990s. JIT, another Japanese innovation, was based on the simple notion that if work was delivered just before it was needed, inventories and costs could be reduced. It is hard to argue with this, but there is a horse-and-cart problem with its implementation.

JIT practitioners assumed that if inventory levels were reduced, problems would be exposed, and people would be motivated to solve them. The image that was often used was that of the water level in a boating reservoir. A high water level (inventory) conceals the rocks (problems). Lowering the water level exposes the rocks so that boaters can avoid or remove them.

Such thinking reverses the arrow of cause and effect. Inventory levels are *results*, not causes. While some are no doubt padded and can be arbitrarily cut, most inventory levels allow for fluctuations in demand and arrival times. To reduce inventory we must first reduce the need for it. Kaoru Ishikawa once observed that if an organization implemented JIT without also implementing SPC, it would simply shut down its operations. What he meant was that if we don't control cycle times, we cannot know how much time to allow for inventory to arrive; and if material arrives "just in time" and it is defective, we must use it or stop work.

Reengineering was an expansion of the basic JIT philosophy. It was purported to address all resources, not just inventory levels. In practice it focused on headcount. The fundamental concept was sound, namely, to reorganize an organization's process in order that it can achieve similar results with fewer resources. But again, the cart was put before the horse.

Managers failed to distinguish between the inputs and the outputs of the reengineering process. They assumed that if they eliminated a lot of people (presumably because there was a great deal of non-value-added activity) the survivors would intuitively stop spending time on wasteful efforts and focus more effectively on truly productive functions. Of course, what the survivors actually spent time on was polishing their resumes.

Not only did management fail to understand the context in which reengineering needed to operate, even the authors of the first book on reengineering, Michael Hammer and James Champy, failed to appreciate the roles of process improvement and strategic planning as integral components of any reengineering effort. According to *The Wall Street Journal* (November 26, 1996), Hammer said in looking back on his 1993 book, "I was reflecting my engineering background and was insufficiently appreciative of the human dimension. I've learned that's critical." The *Journal* continues, "Companies are learning that simply cutting staff, *rather than reorganizing the way people in different functions work*, won't yield the 'quantum leaps' in performance Messrs. Hammer and Champy heralded in their book (emphasis added)."

In short, the promised results of reengineering didn't happen, just as Just-In-Time management didn't entirely meet expectations. In neither case did reducing resources (people in one case, inventory in the other) result in a miraculously superior level of performance.

Strategic Planning — Strategic planning is another management concept that was popular for a while, died out, and then, according to *Business Week* (August 26, 1996), came back. The real drawback to strategic planning is seldom the plan itself, but the failure of management to use the plan to guide significant decisions — in short, to ensure that decisions move the organization toward the goals of its strategic plan. My own experiences with executive teams often revealed that although they had spent significant time and energy developing segments of the plan, the final result was often not accessible. Some typical responses were:

"We helped create the plan, but we never saw the final version (copy)."

"We keep the plan in the vault because of all the sensitive material it contains."

A plan that nobody uses may be called many things, but "strategic" should not be one of them. It is not even clear if it should be called a "plan."

The history of five-year plans and the like has not been encouraging. And yet, without a clear notion of where the organization wants to be, how can management know if they are getting there? Once again, we see the consequences of an important idea executed by rote. The actions are performed, but nothing of significance results.

Guru-Based Systems — During the 1970s, as the West began to recognize the economic achievements of Japan and the influence of Western experts on their successes, various quality "gurus" gained prominence, including Deming, Juran, Crosby and others. Companies would adopt one guru's "philosophy" and try to implement it. Sometimes different groups within a company would adopt different gurus, after which a sort of civil war would develop. I was called in by the General Motors Quality Institute in 1989 to help resolve just such a situation. By laying out the precepts preached by each of the "Battling Gurus," we identified areas of commonality as well as some of differing emphasis. There were actually very few instances of outright contradiction (this exercise was the seedling that eventually grew into our concept of Fusion Management).

The obvious flaw of guru-based management was that few of these gurus actually had a *system*. What they had were philosophies, whether of Breakthrough (Juran), Statistical Thinking (Deming), Zero Defects (Crosby) or Designed Experiments (Taguchi). By itself a philosophy is a good thing to have because it motivates everything else. But it is best if an organization develops its own.

Performance Excellence Awards — Awards such as the Deming Prize in Japan, the European Foundation for Quality Management's (EFQM) European Quality Award (EQA) and the US Malcolm Baldrige National Quality Award (MBNQA), emphasize process and results while avoiding quality philosophy. These awards have evolved over the years, with emphasis gradually shifting from internal processes to business results. In effect, the award is for accomplishment and is largely indifferent as to how the accomplishments are achieved, save only that there must be some evidence that the results are accomplished on purpose. Let's look at the 2002 MBNQA criteria (Figure 1-2).

Performance excellence awards have been increasing in popularity and have a very positive effect on organizations. There are cross-national awards (e.g., EFQM), national awards (e.g., MBNQA) and state and regional awards (e.g., New Jersey's Governor's Award for Performance Excellence). The original list of target organizations included large manufacturing businesses, large service businesses, small manufacturing and services businesses, health care organizations, educational organizations and public agencies. The Presidential Award, for example, recognizes US government agencies that achieve excellence on a point scale using MBNQA criteria. The New Jersey Governor's Award for Performance Excellence includes all the organizational types listed above.

Note that the Deming Prize from Japan was originally used as a baseline in developing the US MBNQA. The Deming Prize depended on consultants to

FIGURE 1-2 COMPARISON OF MBNQA CRITERIA

1988	Maximum Points	2002	Maximum Points
Leadership	150	Leadership	120
Strategic Quality Planning	75	Strategic Planning	85
Customer Satisfaction	300	Customer and Market Focus	85
Information and Analysis	75	Information and Analysis	90
Human Resources Utilization	150	Human Resource Focus	85
QA of Products and Services	150	Process Management	85
Results from QA of P&S	100	Business Results	450
Total Points	**1,000**	**Total Points**	**1,000**

guide companies through the process. Quality New Jersey (QNJ) has borrowed this same concept and actually assists organizations on the journey to excellence. Services provided by QNJ include assisted self-assessment, baseline assessment and award assessment. Fusion Management can also be implemented in a similar fashion.

Award-based systems, unfortunately, are *des*criptive, not *pre*scriptive. They can tell us what a successful organization looks like, but not how to get there. They may be results based but there are few, if any, generally accepted measures of success that transcend industries. Thus, without some structure to accomplish the results, success is achieved idiosyncratically, some companies having won their awards by "sprinting" — that is, by an all-out effort. A few years later, these companies often find themselves not quite as excellent as they once had been because they never had a structure in place for transforming their "sprint" into a "marathon." They were in the position of the jumper who leaped across a chasm without ever building a bridge.

FUSION MANAGEMENT

Since I started my list of 32 *programmes du jour* in 1997, many colleagues have made contributions to it, increasing the total to about 70. In the 70-plus years since Shewhart's 1931 text, we can point to an average of about one new program per year. Over the past 40 years, I have personally observed many of these initiatives. They have focused on improving quality, profitability or productivity, on reducing cycle time or cost and on achieving excellence. Most have contained similar ingredients, but each new program was always hyped as unique, better and different and (almost invariably) as fully supported by top management.

We see many examples of sound management concepts floundering in practice. Sometimes the reason lies in dysfunctional management families, which can strangle even the most promising idea. More often, they flounder because of insufficient understanding, poor deployment, ambiguous goals and measures and short management attention spans. As a result, concepts are discredited and a search for another new management panacea begins. Sometimes the new panacea is simply an older one with a new name.

The problem, of course, is that none of them are *pan*aceas.

Pan is a Greek prefix meaning "universal," and none of the various *programmes du jour* are actually universal. We have seen goals without methods and methods without goals. Techniques have been elevated to the status of programs and programs reduced to mere rote technique. But what if these ideas were considered as facets of a larger whole? What if we could *fuse* them into something that was greater than the sum of its parts? What if choosing which approach to take wasn't an either-or proposition? Then we could combine the motivational aspects of ZD with the cascading goals of MBO and apply the problem-solving methods of SPC (in its broader sense) using QC circles and TQM teams.

Of course the blend that works best will vary from organization to organization. A charitable fund-raising group generally operates a bit differently than a steel mill. The key is to create a single delicious recipe for *excellence* from the many quality cookbooks gathering dust on our shelves.

The *Merriam-Webster's Collegiate Dictionary* defines fusion as "a union by or as if by melting; a merging of diverse, distinct, or separate elements into a unified whole." Fusion cuisine, so popular today in world-class restaurants, refers to blending together diverse flavors, ingredients and national, regional and ethnic cooking styles into a harmonious cuisine. Hence, we refer to our management process as "Fusion Management™."

FUSING WHAT YOU MUST DO WITH WHAT YOU SHOULD DO

We have explored industry's tendency to manage by fad or imitation. Organizations adopt superficial elements of what others have done, without considering whether a particular method is compatible with their own industry, management style, corporate, regional or national culture, or other requirements that have been placed on them.

Our organization once worked with a large contractor in the Midwest, in a highly regulated industry, helping the firm prepare for ISO 9001 registration. At a general planning meeting one of the executives boasted that TQM had been in place for several years, was firmly established and that every worker had the right to stop a process if he or she observed a potential quality issue. One man, a shop steward, raised his hand and politely pointed out that TQM was not really ingrained and that workers rarely spoke out on quality issues. He explained that this was a unionized company, that it was in the Midwest, that it was the primary employer in town, that most of the workers had been there 10 years or longer, that the plant was subject to frequent government and internal audits and that the culture of keeping quiet was too deeply entrenched to change in five years of TQM.

Quite often there is a disconnect between what executives *think* is happening and what *really* is happening. Reality is more complex than a paradigm. That is why Fusion Management requires an examination and evaluation of the systems that an organization already has in place. Only after this has been accomplished do we look at the things an organization *must* do to comply with regulatory requirements, industry standards and customer requirements. We also look at the various tools an organization *should* consider adopting in order to introduce and institutionalize continual improvement into its processes. The final result is a seamlessly fused management system.

Fusion Management is perhaps not so much "different" as it is "more complete" than other programs. In subsequent chapters, we will examine various approaches (strategic–tactical–operational) to Fusion Management and how they compare to each other. We will conclude by presenting a model for developing and deploying a Fusion Management process in your organization.

WHAT'S NEW AND DIFFERENT ABOUT FUSION MANAGEMENT?

There are eight essential characteristics of successful management that are at the heart of our recipe for Fusion Management.

1. The CEO drives the process.
2. The enterprise sets stretch goals.
3. Strategic plans are integrated.
4. Customer requirements are balanced with business results.
5. Key measures of success are tied to the strategic business plan.
6. The management system is process focused.
7. Methods, tools and sequences are designed and fused.
8. Measures of success are tied to the business plan.

1. The CEO drives the process.

Most quality professionals have complained, "If only the CEO would drive this new program…." As discussed earlier, the CEO really can't be committed to driving the process unless he or she truly believes that this is not just another *programme du jour*. But how can one believe this after so many past failures? One thing that captures a senior executive's attention is the testimony of other highly respected CEOs. One reason for the widespread acceptance of Six Sigma, for example, is the preponderance of testimonials from CEOs like Thomas Galvin of Motorola, Jack Welch of GE and Lawrence Bossidy of AlliedSignal/Honeywell (see Chapter 5). The success and widespread acceptance of Six Sigma — internationally, in services as well as in R&D and manufacturing, in both the public and private sectors — is truly a testament to the power of executive commitment. Unfortunately, unless Six Sigma is "fused" into the corporate management systems of these organizations, it will be remembered as just another *programme du jour*.

2. The enterprise sets stretch goals.

Unlike other programs that considered 5 to 10 percent improvements as significant accomplishments, Six Sigma focuses on order of magnitude (10x) breakthrough improvements. In Fusion Management we are interested in both continual improvement (5 to 10 percent) and breakthrough (10x) improvement. Large corporations typically average savings of $250,000 to $350,000 per Six Sigma project. Typically, these corporations employ many project teams, each capable of handling multiple subprojects. The sum of these subprojects constitutes a major opportunity for improvement. When projects are carefully selected and their objectives are clearly stated, they can quickly combine to provide order of magnitude returns.

3. Strategic plans are integrated.

Strategic business plans define who we intend to be and map out the way to achieve our goals. The first step in any strategic plan is to develop the enterprise's "vision." People frequently talk about the CEO's vision, but unless there is a *shared* vision, the probability of attaining it is negligible. The process that the leadership team goes through in crafting the statement is almost as important as the vision statement itself. The vision should be concise and clear and convey the organization's purpose, so that everyone in the organization can visualize the same intent.

Each function or unit then defines its mission. The cumulative effect of completing all these missions is progress toward attaining the enterprise's vision. In many cases, the vision is an image of what the future can be. The missions, meanwhile, are more tangible, which means that we can define metrics that will enable us to gauge our progress towards achieving them. Our vision, in a sense, is a North Star that helps us steer the organization in a constant direction. It helps us answer the question: If we decide to follow this path, are we moving closer to or farther away from our goals? I like to refer to this as a sanity check.

A number of years ago I was working with the senior executive team of a highly successful family-owned business. Shortly after defining the company's vision, the president looked at his brother, a vice president, and said, "We can't go through with the acquisition we've been pursuing." Shocked, the brother asked why. The response was, "It is a lovely toy that we would both like to play with, but it will take us away from where we are trying to go."

By returning to the vision and mission, which are strategic in nature, we continue to cascade through an organization's goals and objectives that are more tactical and shorter in range. Whereas a vision is typically relevant to a company's four-year future, a mission is usually relevant to a company's two-year future. Goals, meanwhile, are usually set on an annual basis and objectives often relate to the next quarter. The enterprise has one vision, each business unit or unique product line may have a mission, each department will have one or more goals and each person may have one or more objectives.

Since we are looking for order of magnitude improvement, we must recognize that change requires creative thinking. Hence, Fusion Management integrates strategic business, quality and regulatory plans. This is discussed more fully in Chapter 4.

4. Customer requirements are balanced with business results.

Every year, *US News and World Report* publishes a guide to America's best colleges. But as Neil George of Webster University points out, the ratings are based almost entirely on measures of input, such as faculty and financial resources, hardly at all on performance (student success rates) and not at all on customer (student/parent) satisfaction. Rather than focusing on internal measures of success and on doing things well — including things that should perhaps be altogether avoided — Fusion Management stresses a balance of internal and external goals as well as short-term and long-range objectives.

The concept of a balanced scorecard is to focus our attention and resources in order to both exceed customer expectations and to achieve significantly higher business results. The tools we use for integrated strategic planning, including the voice of the customer, quality function deployment, failure mode and effects analysis and design of experiments, are all used here.

Fusion Management is about creating "win-win" environments where all the stakeholders come out ahead. Our relationships with customers and suppliers, both internal and external, involve identifying opportunities for improvement that impact our activities and our partners' activities (customers/suppliers) as well.

5. Key measures of success are tied to the strategic business plan.

Fusion Management advocates the use of visual metrics because they enable everyone in an organization to manage business performance and results. In discussing integrated strategic planning, we like to point out the dashboard approach, so called for the automobile display of the key vital signs that are necessary to operate the vehicle safely and efficiently. We need to treat our business in the same manner. Once we have defined the vital signs we will use to run the enterprise, we need to ensure that these measures are readily available. Visual displays such as the dashboard are useful methods to get the "real time" information needed to "steer" the organization.

6. The management system is process focused.

Fusion Management is process focused. Despite the increasing emphasis over the past 50 years on process thinking — process mapping, process validation and cross-functional team activities — this concept still gets buried as organizations get fractionalized by turf wars, inability to "think out of the box," micromanagement and other obstacles to system-level thinking. The remainder of this book emphasizes process issues.

7. Methods, tools and sequences are designed and fused.

In Fusion Management we employ all the tools mentioned thus far — where they apply to our product lines, our corporate culture and our strategic and tactical objectives. The last chapter of this book presents a road map for developing and implementing a Fusion Management process in your organization.

8. Measures of success are tied to the business plan.

Fusion Management focuses on business results. This book aims to highlight what we have learned from past experiences and to demonstrate how we can fuse management system models, Six Sigma and Lean/TQM tools and performance excellence criteria into a comprehensive approach to enterprise knowledge management. We can learn to adopt the most useful features of each new (or old) approach and blend them into our existing management practices. Why throw away our accomplishments every few years just to embrace the latest fad when we can build on them instead?

SUMMARY: COMPETING APPROACHES TO QUALITY

The *pursuit of excellence* is a common theme in many of the quality and business process improvement initiatives introduced over the last half-century. Most of the approaches to improvement fall into three major categories:

1. *Management systems* are based on some set of consensus or regulatory requirements, adherence to which presumably assures a certain minimum acceptable level of quality. Of these, ISO 9000 is currently the most widespread.

2. *Business process improvement strategies* emphasize qualitative and quantitative analytical tools to measure, analyze, improve and control the quality of a product or service. These approaches emphasize effectiveness (improvement in the output of the process) and/or efficiency (improvement in the cycle time and resource usage of the process). TQM and Lean Enterprise are current examples of these. This group also includes Breakthrough Strategies, such as Reengineering (currently out of favor) and Six Sigma (which uses many of the tools of TQM), which strive for order-of-magnitude improvements in business results.

3. *Performance excellence models* use a set of award criteria to evaluate both the elements of a quality management system and the business results provided by that system. These tend to be national or regional in their scope — the Malcolm Baldrige National Quality Award (MBNQA) and the European Quality Award (EQA) being among the most widely known.

In subsequent chapters we will examine and compare the major trends in management systems, business process improvement and performance excellence, beginning with the evolution of structured management systems.

2
Managing What We Do

ORIGINS OF QUALITY MANAGEMENT SYSTEMS

The earliest quality standards — process specifications and product specifications — date back to ancient times. For example, the Ebers Papyrus (ancient Egypt, ca. 1500 BC) contains a number of pharmaceutical process specifications. Kings and pharaohs set standards of weights and measures for all craftsmen in the kingdom. In Egypt, the "golden cubit," based on the length of the forearm, was kept in the pharaoh's palace and all builders were required to bring their cubit sticks to the palace annually to be verified. Calibration requirements of this sort (without the pharaoh) are still found in management system standards today, and the authority to set standards for weights and measures is one of the enumerated duties of the executive branch in the US Constitution.

For the most part, however, individual craftsmen set their own standards of quality. These craftsmen were in daily contact with their customers and would design, manufacture and assure the quality of their own products. Their marketplace was considerably smaller: sometimes the village itself, at other times, regional fairs or nearby market towns. Very often, the craftsman knew the customer personally and, more important, the customer and everyone else in the village knew the craftsman. Poor design and execution errors had direct and personal consequences, and as a result, they received direct and personal attention.

In Europe during the Middle Ages, an industrial revolution, powered by wind and water, greatly expanded the scope of industry. A lively international trade developed. Rhenish glass, Flemish cloth and English wool were among those products that gained reputations for high quality thousands of miles from their origins. Textile workers in Flanders were gathered together to practice their craft "in company." In some cases this led to great strife; for example, in 1274 the weavers and fullers of Ghent left their city en masse to go to the neighboring Duchy of Brabant, whose duke had promised better wages and conditions.

All of this required more complex management than the self-employed village craftsman. It was one thing to manage your own work; it was quite another to manage the coordinated work of many others. Such new demands gave rise to new tools. Among them were management audits, an example of which survives in a report on the management of the work at the great Cathedral of York. In it, the auditor describes such familiar problems as unfit workmen, building defects and unsuitable machinery. The report, copied below, could have been written today and the issues described — internal audits, training, corrective action and the use of suitable equipment — are still requirements for any good management system.

REPORT ON THE MANAGEMENT OF THE WORKS AT YORK MINSTER, 9-12 JANUARY 1345

[The Master of the Works] … says that once he paid Roger de Hirton, mason of the fabric, his wages for almost a fortnight, when he was absent all the time and had done no work. … Also there was often removal of timber stone and lime, and [he] knows not where it went. The roofing of the church and the stonework suffer injury through lack of care… The wardens of the work and also the workmen, though they seemed to be capable, often quarreled, so that the work was often delayed and is endangered. The outer pilasters, which are called buttresses, have for the most part perished for defect of covering. Also W. the carpenter is an old man and cannot work at high levels. It is ordered that a younger man be employed in his place and that the old man shall supervise defects.

The Master of the Masons appeared 11 January. He says that there are many of the masons who go against his orders and also workmen who are not capable or fit for their work and that some are so disobedient that he cannot restrain or punish them properly. Also that timber, stone, lime, cement and so forth have frequently been made away with; and that there has been much misappropriation of stone from the quarry and that almost nothing fit for work is brought in. For lack of proper care and of roofing there is such a quantity of water that lately a lad has almost been drowned; and these defects arise from the lack of lead roofing. Also he says that he cannot look after the work, workmen and other things as he ought, because he is interfered with by the Mayor, and he cannot view defects because Sir Thomas de Ludham alone has the keys to the door of the fabric.

11 January. Will. de Wrsal, Under-master of the Works, says that the chief defect that he knows is that the cranes at the west end of the church are rotten and worthless. The Master of Carpenters says that he does not know of any maladministration by the chamberlain except that he occasionally gives away stone, and he thinks he received money for the gift. Also he thinks that the chamber which Richard de Melton made beside the church is useless and very injurious to the work and ought to be removed.

Account reprinted in *The Medieval Machine*, Jean Gimpel, Holt, Rinehart and Winston (New York, 1976).

While it may be comforting to know that management in the 14th century had many of the same problems that we have today, it is also troublesome to see that after six and a half centuries we still have them.

MODERN DEVELOPMENTS

The concept of "division of labor" was described by Adam Smith in his 1776 work, *The Wealth of Nations*, and was applied by French textile mills and Eli Whitney's New England gun shops in the early 1800s. Rather than have each craftsman produce the entire product, with the result that no two items were sufficiently alike as to be interchangeable, the work was divided into several tasks, with each craftsman assigned to one specific job. Because each craftsman performed the same task repeatedly, it was thought that their output would become more and more alike, reducing the need for selective assembly. However, since there was always some variation from piece to piece, Whitney allowed "tolerances" to be set around the target value. He would tell the craftsmen what they were supposed to achieve and the craftsmen would apply their skills to achieve it.

In the 1880s, close to 90 percent of the people of the United States and Great Britain were engaged in three occupational categories: agriculture, domestic service and equestrian occupations. A century later, only about 2 percent were so employed. This does not mean there was massive unemployment; what happened was a massive shift from an agricultural economy to a manufacturing one. Similar shifts occurred across Europe and, later, in nations like Japan.

The influx of "farm boys and women" into the new steam-powered, urban factories presented managers with a work force that did not possess the skills of trained craftsmen. Consequently, in the late 1880s, Frederick Winslow Taylor, an American mechanical engineer, pushed the idea of "scientific management." Faced with a pool of poorly educated immigrants, Taylor broke tasks down to their simplest elements, reasoning that even an unskilled worker could be taught to perform these motions and tasks.

The Taylor system of management accomplished many good things. Productivity soared. The quality was mediocre compared to the handmade product of the craftsman, but at least it was affordable. Items that had previously been available only to the well-to-do suddenly became available to the masses. Henry Ford's Model T is a notable example. Furthermore, Taylor established some valuable principles. As enumerated by Juran, these principles included:

❖ Methods for measuring work and analyzing jobs.

❖ Matching workers to jobs through job specifications and training.

❖ Specific and clearly understood goals.

Less happily, Taylor separated the planning from the doing of work. Managers and engineers would make the plans; the foremen and workers would carry them out. "Under our system," he once wrote, "a workman is told just what he is to do and how to do it. Any improvement he makes upon the orders given him is fatal to his success." There was, Taylor asserted in what became a slogan of the "efficiency movement," *one right way to do a job*. The workman was not simply given a target and a tolerance, as the factory craftsman had been given, but also detailed instructions on how to accomplish the outcome.

This approach increased product uniformity, but there was a downside. Not only were workers told to "check your brains at the door," but because they knew only the one limited task that they were taught to perform, they lost sight of the quality of the finished article. The foreman assumed responsibility for the overall quality of work.

Under the Taylor system workers were paid by the piece, so manufacturing had an incentive to pass anything of marginal quality — or even to pass outright defectives. Independent inspectors were added to counter this, but since every rejected piece meant wages out of the workman's pocket, this was hardly a recipe for a happy workplace. By the 1920s and 1930s, this evolution was almost complete. Inspection and test functions were expanded and separated from production. Manufacturing was no longer responsible for the quality of the product it made.

The Quality Disconnect

During the 20th century, corporations replaced proprietorships and partnerships as the dominant form of business and a rupture developed — not only between producer and customer but also within the ranks of the enterprise itself.

When an islander carved a canoe for his nephew, he made sure it was a darned good canoe. He knew the fisherman who would paddle it, and everybody in the village knew who carved it. This, however, was not the case for a machine operator making a precursor to a part for a subassembly to a final product sold to a merchant who would offer it to a faceless public. As in the case of piecework, there was a built-in incentive to settle marginal cases in favor of immediate and local pressures, such as the need to achieve a quota or fill an order. People always respond more readily to immediate and personal consequences than to the delayed and abstract.

Consequently, the executives of large businesses are at the mercy of the expedient judgments of those farther down the ranks — as was the case in the Bhopal tragedy, when a machine operator at a Union Carbide chemical plant in India ignored corporate safety policies, resulting in the release of a poisonous gas that killed thousands. Executives often exacerbate this tendency by setting up contradictory and conflicting goals and measures that lead to such expedient decisions.

A machinist who worked on the Apollo capsules recalls how NASA combated this problem by returning to the village approach. Astronauts were introduced to the machinists and others who worked on their capsules, and they spent a great deal of time in the shops with them discussing problems. The astronauts developed a personal relationship with their suppliers, and as a result, the suppliers took extra pains to ensure quality and reliability. Unfortunately, this option is not always available, especially in the case of mass-marketed consumer goods.

During the 20th century, the concepts of Taylorism spread from industry to government. Fascist, socialist and communist states experimented with the notion that a small group of planners could set all the rules and the average citizen would be "told just what he is to do and how to do it." The explicit program of the Progressive movement of late 19th and early 20th century America was to apply the methods of "the rational factory" to the governance of the state. The experts would set up the rules and everyone else would comply.

In democratic states, this trend was coupled with good intentions. The idea that a meat packer, for example, could prosper by making its customers sick is ludicrous; yet, there were (and are) many who cut corners out of shortsightedness. It is small comfort to the injured that the responsible organization will probably go out of business in the future. As large corporations became disconnected from their customers, regulators began to act as the quality control inspection department.

Power thus shifted from millions of independent decision makers to government regulators. Laws, regulations, guidelines and consensus standards crept into our lives, and a mind-set began to develop that government should protect its citizens by setting quality standards, at least where health, safety, welfare or national interests are involved. Sometimes these efforts were well conceived and resulted in easier and safer lives, but sometimes not. Government managers are no more astute than their corporate counterparts; they are no more connected to the customer, and they are certainly just as capable of inappropriate or ineffective actions. Although they are presumably immune to the profit motive as a reason to cut corners, they are also immune to the profit motive as a reason to satisfy and delight customers. Thus, when industry fails or lacks the resources to act effectively and health, safety, or national interests are at stake — as in the case of airport safety and security — we can expect the government to intervene, possibly at the expense of not only profit but also customer satisfaction.

Protections that were established in the 19th century to guard against *fraudulent* business practices were broadened in the 20th century. For example, a constitutional amendment gave the federal government authority to regulate alcoholic beverages. While that amendment was later repealed, no one asks today where the authority comes from to regulate drugs other than alcohol. The US Constitution also expressly charges the executive branch with the authority to set standards of weights and measures. This function was first performed by the Bureau of Weights and Measures and later placed within a broader Department of Commerce, only to become the National Bureau of Standards and finally the National Institute of Standards and Technology, which today operates a wide variety of programs, including the Malcolm Baldrige National Quality Award.

The US federal government employs more than 2.5 million civilians working in 13 major departments and more than 60 agencies, boards, commissions and government corporations, many of them with some quality-related oversight function. For example, the US Department of Agriculture enforces uniform safeguards and standards of quality for the food supply. The Food and Drug Administration of the Department of Health and Human Services sets standards for adulteration or mislabeling of foods, drugs, medical devices and cosmetics. The Department of Labor is responsible for, among other matters, the occupational safety and health of workers.

Perhaps the government's deepest involvement in the quality of goods and services came about as a result of the needs of defense and aerospace.

QUALITY SYSTEMS IN DEFENSE AND AEROSPACE

During World War II, the government itself became a major purchaser of goods and services and, as any large customer, issued quality specifications for the products it purchased. Occasionally these specifications resulted in unnecessarily expensive hammers and toilet seats, but more often they reflected special performance requirements. For example, a coffee maker fit for use in an airplane that flies at high altitudes and engages in steep dives and climbs is something that the government cannot pick up at the local appliance shop.

Looking to make sense out of a plethora of individual product specifications, military procurement people hit upon the notion of a quality *system* standard. A company may produce good products by accident or on purpose. If by accident, then expensive sorting, rework or other unnecessary costs would be incurred in order to *deliver* good quality. (First you make a lot of defects; then you hunt for them and fix them.) This is obviously more expensive than not making the defects in the first place. The government did not wish to absorb such costs so it came up with a set of fundamental management practices to which suppliers would adhere. With such guidelines in place, the government would have some assurance that good quality was produced "on purpose." This approach would reduce the need for detailed product inspections by substituting, in part, a detailed inspection of the contractor's procedures and practices.

Having learned some painful lessons during World War II, the government mandated rigorous quality standards in the "Cold War" era. The Department of Defense (DoD) issued the first quality system requirements in 1959 with Military Specification MIL-Q-9858, "Quality Program Requirements," later amended as MIL-Q-9858A. Success, especially in reducing inspection workloads, led to copycat standards as other agencies created their own versions. Three years later, the National Aeronautics and Space Administration (NASA) introduced NASA Quality Publication NPC 200-2, "Quality Program

Provisions for Space System Contractors." A nuclear quality system require-ment followed in 1969, and the Consumer Product Safety Commission (CPSC) issued the "Handbook and Standard for Manufacturing Safer Consumer Products" in 1975. Various standards in the United States and elsewhere, such as Canadian National Standard Z299, addressed the same requirements by and large but, as with any process of copy-and-repeat, particular differences accu-mulated. Sometimes these were editorial in nature to address the language of the industry or field with a particular style of writing. For example, MIL-Q-9858A refers to "contractors" and is couched in mandatory language, while the CPSC Handbook refers to "manufacturers" and expresses itself as recommen-dations. The former deals with contractual requirements, whereas the latter merely issues recommended guidelines.

My own career as a quality professional parallels the increased use of such system standards. In 1960, while completing a bachelor's degree in applied sta-tistics, I was interviewed for a job by a retired admiral who was the shipyard superintendent for the General Dynamics Electric Boat Co. in Groton, Connecticut, which was building nuclear submarines for the US Navy. A crusty sort, the admiral conducted a brief interview, glanced at my paperwork and said, "I have no idea what a statistician is supposed to do, but the Navy's head of quality says I need one, and your paperwork says you are one, so the job is yours if you want it. You just have to figure out what the job is." Being young and fool-ish, and not having the foggiest notion of what a quality control statistician did, I took the job — mostly because it paid 10 percent more than all the job offers my classmates at the City College of New York had received at that point!

The first few months were uneventful, until one day the shipyard superin-tendent called me into his office and announced, "I now know why I need a statistician. The Department of Defense has issued a new standard, MIL-Q-9858, which requires that we have a documented quality system. We never had this requirement before, nor have we had a quality control statistician before. Ergo, the task of complying with this requirement is obviously something you should do."

I started this task immediately and began the process of differentiating between the multiple levels of required documentation (manual, procedures and instructions). It quickly became evident that the hierarchical nature of these documents was an important feature, so we developed what is today the well-known pyramid described in Figure 2-1.

I was very fortunate that the Navy's former head of quality, Louis I. Korn, was there to help me. Louis became my first mentor at Electric Boat. He was

FIGURE 2-1 QUALITY MANAGEMENT SYSTEM STRUCTURE

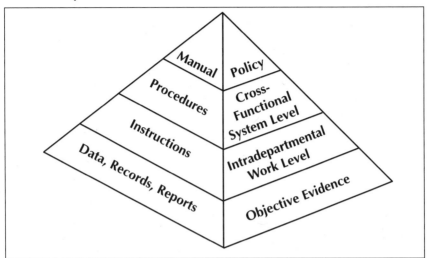

also my first employee when I started STAT-A-MATRIX in 1968, and he remained part of the STAT-A-MATRIX team until he died in February 2002 at 89 years of age.

While we were still developing this management system, the US Navy imposed another standard, MIL-Q-21459, which was a quality system requirement specifically developed for the Navy's Fleet Ballistic Missile (FBM) program. Other FBM contractors, like Lockheed and Westinghouse, were receiving the same requirements. This program, also known as Polaris (later Poseidon and currently Trident), involved the launching of torpedoes from nuclear submarines that could cruise submerged for as long as six months. Obviously, the requirements for reliability and quality were extremely stringent and the potential consequence of failure devastating, as we saw with the tragic events aboard the Russian nuclear submarine, *Kursk*.

One new FBM requirement, for example, was that member organizations had to perform rigid internal audits of their processes. So, in 1961, we developed what was one of the first comprehensive internal quality auditing programs. The program was so successful that we were asked to replicate it in 1962 for the Argonne National Laboratory's Knolls Atomic Power Laboratory in Idaho. These two sites (Connecticut and Idaho) were very early examples of quality management system deployment and audit.

By the mid-1960s, NASA had added NPC 200-2, a requirement for a distinct quality plan to be used with each NASA support project. Unlike the military standards, which required that one overall quality management system cover all products for delivery to DoD, NASA required a *separate* quality plan *specific* to each of its task orders. NASA suppliers needed to demonstrate a detailed plan that started with the product specifications and described the specific steps to be taken to procure appropriate materials and supplies. Next, suppliers had to ensure the quality of the materials and process to achieve the end product. Then they were required to verify that the product met all of the specifications and finally to control the packing and shipping of the product so that it would be received by the prime contractor in its intended condition. In part, NASA developed this requirement so that if some disaster befell a particular supplier, the quality plan could be taken to an alternative supplier who could, in theory, produce the required product based on the contents of the plan.

By the time this NASA standard was released, I had been recruited to work as a statistician for RCA. Within a month I was promoted to head up the quality department for the Memory Products Operation. (I replaced the man who had originally recruited me. Needless to say, he wasn't too happy about it.) The Memory Products Operation made the computer memories for DoD and NASA to support US rocket programs. In those days the computer equivalent of a personal digital assistant (PDA) occupied a space roughly the size of a four-drawer filing cabinet.

Due to the nature of NASA's space missions, a typical order was for three units: one to test to destruction, one to fly the mission and one for backup. Hence, we received many orders for three units and, consequently, had to provide a separate quality plan for each order. At the time, our management team was convinced that we were going to have to develop a new and unique quality plan for each procurement. Technically, this was true, but by recognizing that we had documented, verified and *controlled* processes that were repeated for each order, we could follow one process map and make appropriate modifications to technical requirements and specifications to customize each quality plan. This approach became normal procedure for writing quality plans.

These approaches to quality management systems, along with many of the statistical measurement and prediction techniques that aerospace and defense contractors were developing to meet the emerging requirements of global defense and space exploration, soon migrated to other sectors and became the basis for the ISO 9000 requirements of the last decade.

QUALITY SYSTEMS FOR THE COMMERCIAL NUCLEAR POWER INDUSTRY

In the late 1960s and early 1970s, the Atomic Energy Commission (AEC), now known as the Nuclear Regulatory Commission (NRC), took note of the growing number of nuclear power plants and began to think about a quality system requirement. While some architectural and engineering firms had adopted the military standard MIL-Q-9858 and imposed its requirements on suppliers, the AEC felt that DoD's requirements were not sufficiently stringent or specific for their needs. Therefore, they requested that US standards-writing organizations prepare a consensus standard. The industry agreed to take this on, but more than a year passed without progress.

The AEC then took its own action, entrusting a much smaller group to develop a requirement, which then became part of the US Code of Federal Regulations (CFR). In 1969, the AEC issued a draft of 10 CFR 50 Appendix B, Part 10-Energy, "Quality Assurance Criteria for Nuclear Power Plants," for review prior to issuance, in accordance with standard procedures for CFRs. The industry urged the AEC not to publish the final version and to wait for the industry's consensus standard. The AEC, however, adopted the regulation in 1970, without waiting for the industry standard. A year later the industry standard — American National Standards Institute (ANSI) N45.2 "Quality Assurance Program Requirements for Nuclear Power Plants" — was published, effectively creating two system standards for commercial nuclear power plants.

By the end of 1971, the nuclear power industry had a *third* quality system standard, namely, American Society of Mechanical Engineers NA4000, "ASME Boiler and Pressure Vessel Code, Section III, Division I, Subsection NA, Rules for Construction of Nuclear Power Plant Components, Quality Assurance." The foreword to ANSI N45.2 explains its relationships to the other two standards and illustrates how during the 1960s and 1970s both government and industry were groping their way toward a workable process for creating such standards.

In 1972, I chaired a panel discussion introducing ANSI N45.2 and relating it to 10 CFR 50 Appendix B. The panel consisted of representatives from AEC, ANSI's standards developers, architectural engineers and contractors. The panel was presented at the then American Society for Quality Control's (ASQC) annual conference and was attended by more than 600 people. It was repeated in the same month at the annual meeting of the American Nuclear Society (ANS). In the following years, additional standards proliferated, some of them as add-ons to N45.2. This was the result of the decision by the standards committee to establish a single high-level document and supplement it with more detailed standards referred to as "daughter documents." This policy was adopted to be able to publish new standards rapidly. The 23 planned documents were numbered N45.2.1 to N45.2.23 and covered such diverse areas as packaging and storage, cleaning, housekeeping, calibration and control of measuring and test equipment, record keeping and auditing — in short, many of the items that were in MIL-Q-9858 and later in ISO 9001.

By the early 1980s, it became clear to the nuclear industry that the proliferation of quality requirements was creating a great deal of confusion. After many meetings, it was agreed that a single consolidated consensus standard, ANSI/ASME NQA-1, would replace the previously issued documents and that compliance with NQA-1 would be accepted by the AEC (NRC) as equivalent to compliance with 10 CFR 50 Appendix B.

RELATED DEVELOPMENTS IN THE FDA

Meanwhile, in the late 1960s, the US Food and Drug Administration (FDA) introduced the concept of Good Manufacturing Practices (GMP) to the US Code of Federal Regulations. The GMPs applied quality systems requirements to suppliers of FDA-regulated items. Ultimately, there was one GMP for medical devices, one for pharmaceuticals and a third for food handling, processing and packaging. All three dealt with buildings, facilities and equipment as well as issues of quality control, treaceability, recall, cleanliness, sanitation, foreign bodies, segregation of defective products and related matters. The pharmaceutical GMP addresses a number of other quality-related areas such as organization and personnel, control of components and drug product containers and closures, production and process control, packaging and labeling controls, holding and distribution, laboratory controls, records, reports and returned and salvaged drug products.

Congress created the FDA in 1906 to address adulteration of food and drugs. In 1938, cosmetics were added to the agency's responsibilities and, in 1976, medical devices. The latter was sufficiently unique that past practice proved insufficient. Different knowledge and experience were needed, both to develop the medical device requirements and to perform the required inspections and audits. Furthermore, investigators skilled in pharmaceuticals or food needed training to adjust to the processes and methods used in the medical device industry.

My experiences with DoD, NASA and AEC had shown that if large companies used these system standards to improve their business processes (rather than to gain a new lobby plaque), they would achieve great economic benefits. Because the standards define the core activities essential to achieving customer satisfaction, they could be used to identify and eliminate a great deal of non-value-added work. These "lessons learned" were incorporated into the STAT-A-MATRIX course "Quality Program Preparation and Audit," a popular pre-ISO 9000 course that described how implementing a quality management system would benefit even a nonregulated organization through increased efficiency, reduced cycle time, improved quality and optimized cost.

During the 1970s, a substantial number of FDA personnel had taken this course and, as a result, I was invited to help develop the new Medical Device Good Manufacturing Practice (GMP), 21 CFR 820. In particular, I helped ensure that the Economic Impact Statement, which the FDA was required to file on new regulations, included these benefits in its analysis. In the spring of 1978, I worked with a group of FDA executives, FDA investigators and other industry experts to present and explain the new Medical Device GMP to over 2,000 FDA and industry personnel in 12 cities in six weeks!

We recognized that compliance might initially be more difficult for small companies. It costs about as much for a small company to comply with a given requirement as it does for a large company. This observation was significant because, unlike food, pharmaceuticals and cosmetics, a large percentage of registered medical device firms were, and still are, small companies. To help smaller firms become compliant, the FDA created the Office of Small Manufacturers Assistance (OSMA).

CODES, REGULATIONS AND STANDARDS

We have seen how four diverse government agencies — DoD, NASA, AEC and FDA — found it useful to establish management system requirements to ensure the quality of products and services where life, safety and security are primary issues. Reliable military equipment is vital to the safety of military personnel and to those whom they are sworn to protect. For NASA, a major goal is manned space flight and, in the early 1960s, many rocket trials failed badly. The FDA's mission is to ensure the quality, safety and cleanliness of foods, drugs and medical products and the AEC oversees the safety of nuclear power plants. While DoD and NASA are direct purchasers of products, the FDA and AEC are not customers, but third-party "quality control assessors" acting on behalf of the public.

FIGURE 2-2 HIERARCHY OF REQUIREMENTS

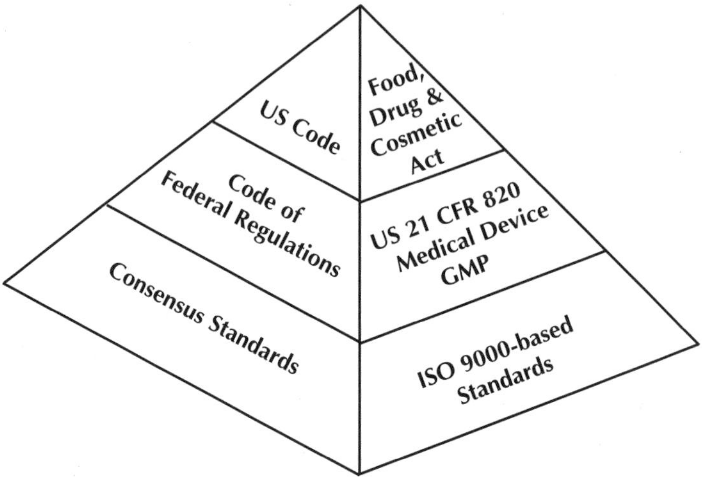

The hundreds of government standards that resulted from these efforts, including MIL-Q-9858A, MIL-Q-21459, NPC 200-2 and various CFRs, were specifications imposed for government procurements or regulatory processes. DoD and NASA requirements represented conditions for procurement and were accepted as contractual requirements when the supplier agreed to accept the contract. They were formulated in the absence of industry consensus standards — there were no legal private customers for military systems or manned spacecraft — but when an acceptable commercial specification existed, the government standard would often refer to it. In recent years, in an attempt to "harmonize" international requirements and reduce costs, military and NASA standards have been replaced by commercial standards, where possible, and the ISO and ANSI hierarchy of standards has been expanded to meet such needs.

The US Code of Federal Regulations is the government's way of notifying people that a regulatory body (such as the FDA) has proposed a requirement. Figure 2-2 illustrates the relationship between three distinct sets of requirements — United States Code (the law), Code of Federal Regulations (interpretation of the law) and consensus standards (accepted by mutual agreement).

US Code (Laws) — As part of its lawmaking activities, Congress creates laws and may establish regulatory agencies to ensure that the laws are effectively implemented. For example, Congress created the FDA to regulate food and drugs and, later, cosmetics and medical devices. The AEC was created to regulate nuclear energy. Products that the government directly acquires (for the

DoD or NASA) are also governed by the Federal Acquisition Regulations (FARs), which form part of the US Code.

Code of Federal Regulations — When Congress created agencies such as the FDA and the AEC, it gave them the power to promulgate documents in the form of sections of the Code of Federal Regulations (CFR). These regulations have the force of law since they interpret the law and define how it should be enforced; however, enforcement is through the US Code.

Consensus Standards — By the mid-1960s, DoD had thousands of military standards covering everything from bicycles to canned foods to weapon systems. By the 1970s, many trade associations and professional societies were creating similar standards for commercial items. Consider for a moment the plug used to connect an electric appliance to a power supply. There are at least seven configurations and multiple levels of current and voltage for electrical connectors of home appliances, most of them incompatible. The differences around the world for a simple plug, as well as varying voltage and current standards, present major obstacles to international trade.

Consensus standards for products are designed to minimize such differences and to standardize products around a minimal number of configurations so that common parts are interchangeable throughout the world and common products are globally functional. Similarly, consensus standards for quality management systems assure that products anywhere in the world are produced under a minimal set of required good management practices.

MOVEMENT TOWARD ISO 9000

In 1968, NATO introduced a three-part quality system requirement: the Allied Quality Assurance Publication (AQAP)-1, 2 and 3, based in part on MIL-Q-9858A. This document established quality requirements for three different levels of quality assurance. Based on the AQAPs, in 1979, the British Standards Institution adopted a consensus standard, BS5750, that contained an approach similar to the NATO quality system to address the requirements for a quality management system. This approach also focused on three possible levels of quality assurance:

❖ Level 1: Design, manufacturing and distribution.

❖ Level 2: Manufacturing and distribution.

❖ Level 3: Distribution.

The Canadian National Standard Z299, which followed, had four levels:

- ❖ 1: Quality Assurance Program Requirements.
- ❖ 2: Quality Control Program Requirements.
- ❖ 3: Quality Verification Program Requirements.
- ❖ 4: Inspection Program Requirements.

Each level or part described a management system of increasing (or decreasing) complexity. This system set up a "ladder" for a company to climb. Not every organization did design work, and mass production of consumer goods was different from one-of-a-kind, contract-specific construction. The more weight given to control, the less needed for inspection, and the more weight given to planning, the less needed for both control and inspection. As one quality manager said in describing the evolution of his plastic injection molding company, "First, we were a 'squirt-and-ship' shop. Then we became a 'squirt-inspect-and-ship' shop. Now we are a 'control-squirt-inspect-and-ship' shop. One day, we hope to become a 'plan-control-squirt-inspect-and-ship' shop."

Third-party schemes evolved in the 1960s. During this time, defense and nuclear regulations required each procuring agency or prime contractor to audit its suppliers. This resulted in multiple and conflicting audits, with resulting cost and distraction. For example, in 1964, when I was a quality manager for an RCA division that supplied computer-related systems, it was not unusual to find two or three military-related customers auditing our facilities at the same time, even though DoD contracts accounted for only 5 percent of our business! Because of this burden, large defense contractors created a cooperative effort known as CASE (Coordinated Aerospace Supplier Evaluation), which was a precursor to third-party schemes. CASE would eliminate redundant audits by pooling audit results. Each CASE participant would have access to the system audits performed by other participants on the same supplier. These audits would be prepared in a standard report format and placed in a database. Thus, customer X could satisfy part of the regulatory requirement to audit its suppliers by citing the audit report of customer Y. (Compliance with specific technical and performance requirements of the product, often proprietary, was another matter, which still required product-specific reviews.)

During the 1970s a similar development arose in the US commercial nuclear industry, when several companies cooperated to reduce the costs and distractions of multiple audits. Initially two companies — one on the East Coast and one in the Midwest — agreed to perform audits for each other. Either company could request the other to perform an audit for them, and any audit done by either organization would be made available to the other. Over time, more and more companies joined the cooperative, and the records of approved companies continued to grow. The nuclear industry was also the first to adopt industry-specific standards for the performance of audits and the certification of lead auditors: ANSI N45.2.12 and ANSI N45.2.23 — two of the "daughter standards" to ANSI N45.2 referred to earlier.

To reduce the number of audits to which suppliers would be subjected, the British introduced an *independent* (or *"third-party"*) *assessment scheme* in place of the bewildering variety of second-party and industry-specific schemes. The British Standards Institution (BSI) established criteria for auditor certification based on ANSI N45.2-23, which required candidates to (1) take an auditing course, (2) pass an examination, (3) possess other education and experience detailed in a combined point system and (4) complete a specified number of audits. BSI also introduced a quality system standard (BS5750), and its auditor requirements later became the basis of ISO 10011, which has been superseded by ISO 19011.

Today, the International Organization for Standardization (ISO), headquartered in Geneva, Switzerland, is the repository for many international consensus standards, with over 100 nations represented. In some respects, ISO operates like the United Nations. Each country sends a delegation to attend meetings, where various working groups define parts of the standards under development. Each delegation develops a national consensus with other relevant groups, such as professional societies, and brings a national position to the general meetings. These meetings rotate among various host countries, so that each region of the world will find at least some meetings close to home. This practice enables more organizations to participate in the process.

Most ISO standards were written to ensure the compatibility of products (for example, the ISO standard for photographic film speeds). In the mid-1980s, ISO formed Technical Committee (TC) 176 to begin work on global standards for quality management and quality assurance systems that could be used commercially (where regulatory requirements didn't apply). The result was the ISO 9000 family of standards, which was first published in 1987 and revised in 1994 and 2000. These standards include many of the same requirements found in earlier defense and nuclear standards. Indeed, sections of the original 1987 version of ISO 9001 were nearly verbatim excerpts of MIL-Q-9858A, the granddaddy of them all. Some regulated industries have adopted the ISO standards, usually with the addition of industry-specific requirements.

FIGURE 2-3 COMPARISON OF STANDARDS

Element	MIL-Q-9858A	10 CFR 50 Appendix B	ANSI N45.2	ISO 9001:2000	FDA Device GMP	FDA Drug GMP
Organization	X	X	X	X	X	X
QA Planning	X	X	X	X	X	X
Design Control	X	X	X	X	*	*
Documented Procedures	X	X	X	X	X	X
Document Control	X	X	X	X	X	X
Control of Purchased Products	X	X	X	X	X	X
Traceability	X	X	X	X	X	X
Process Control	*	*	*	X	X	X
Control of Special Processes	X	X	X	X	X	*
Inspection	X	X	X	X	X	X
Test Control	X	X	X	X	X	X
Control of Test Equipment	X	X	X	X	X	X
Handling, Storage and Shipping	X	X	X	X	X	X
Inspection and Test Status	X	X	X	X	X	X
Nonconforming Materials	X	X	X	X	X	X
Corrective Action	X	X	X	X	X	X
QA Records	X	X	X	X	X	X
Audits	*	X	X	X	X	*
Quality Cost	X	*	*	*	*	*
Quality Training	*	*	*	X	X	X
SPC	X	*	*	X	X	X

Note: X indicates that the standard specifically addresses this element.
     * indicates that the standard does not specifically address this element.

There is little in the requirements of ISO 9001:2000 that a savvy executive would not want to see in practice in his or her organization. For example, Clause 7.4.2, Purchasing Information, states: "Purchasing information shall describe the product to be purchased...." In other words: "Whenever you buy something, tell the seller what you want." It is difficult to imagine any manager issuing a purchase order without stating what is being purchased. It is, however, easy to imagine unclear, partial or incorrect information in a purchasing transaction. This is what makes the standard more than a list of truisms for executives. It spells out the essentials and asks that the organization have some means of ensuring that the essentials are met. For example, how *does* your organization make certain that purchase order information is correct and complete and understood by your supplier? Figure 2-3 compares some of the key quality standards.

BEYOND COMPLIANCE

One problem with government-imposed systems, as perceived by industry, is the excessive level of documentation required by regulators whose mission is to assure that industry has complied with a particular set of requirements. After the FDA's Good Manufacturing Practices were imposed, affected companies reported that the GMPs cost them money. Some firms complained of the added costs of documentation and audits or of having to hire additional staff to comply with the requirements. These companies were generally those that chose to comply on a strict command-and-control basis. They did not approach the standards as a compendium of good business practices to be studied and implemented. The companies that chose the system-improvement route acknowledged that the discipline of a common standard was useful and ultimately resulted in savings. They found that the *process of implementation*, including, as it did, a thorough study and analysis of all operations addressed by the standard, helped streamline their businesses and led to returns on their investments.

The movement, since the late 1980s, toward internationally recognized consensus standards was intended to "harmonize" various international standards and to eliminate the redundancies and inconsistencies of many disparate standards. A major problem, for example, was that of suppliers working in several industries with multiple clients. For example, a supplier selling electronic components used in aerospace, automobiles and medical devices — a common situation — would be forced to maintain three distinct quality systems and to undergo DoD and FDA audits as well as audits by various major customers. The supplier might have three different documentation and reporting systems.

Further, the service portions of the supplier's processes, often as important as the original product, were frequently excluded from the system requirements.

These consensus standards, however, represent a *minimum* set of requirements, not an optimum and not a maximum. To achieve consensus, all member bodies must participate, and a significant portion of the voting members (typically 70 to 90 percent) must approve. However, member bodies will vary in their degree of sophistication and those with fewer resources are unlikely to vote themselves into a competitive disadvantage. Even sophisticated member bodies dislike placing restrictions on themselves that are not needed to achieve the purpose of the standard. This is as true of nations agreeing upon an international standard as it is of companies agreeing upon a sector-specific standard within a particular industry.

In describing the recall of 6.5 million Bridgestone/Firestone Wilderness tires, *USA Today* referred to ISO 9000 as a "rigid quality standard" ("Quality Auditor OK'd Decatur Tire Plant," Sept. 8, 2000). The person who said this was mistaken. The ISO 9000 family of standards is anything but rigid and defines only the critical activities a quality *management system* must encompass. It is not by any means a standard for tires, or any other product. Even an outstanding management system does not guarantee against slipups and design or manufacturing defects.

The article further stated, "A plant making life preservers of cement could get certified." This statement is, of course, as was previously pointed out, a half-truth. If a customer, for some bizarre reason, specified that it wanted to purchase cement life preservers, a plant could get certified while making them, but the standard really is transparent to the product. It requires only that the producer of the goods or services understand what the customer needs and then undertake to produce and deliver those goods or services. The *real* issue is the need to clearly distinguish between product certification and system certification.

A second article in the same issue of *USA Today* reported, "An internal company memo dated January 9, 2000, showed that tread separation incidents cost the company $3 million in 1999, and that Decatur-made tires caused a disproportionate 62 percent of that, or $1.8 million. That was 4.5 times as much as the next-worst plant." The article goes on to state, "The bad Decatur tires mainly were produced in 1994-1996, coinciding with a strike there." The crucial questions regarding the management system are: Why did it take four to six years to recognize there was a problem of whatever origin? And given the January memo, why did it take seven months for the company to react? These questions have implications that go beyond the tire problem. The lesson to be learned is that even the most powerful engine (or management system) will go nowhere if you do not put it in gear. The Decatur plant was closed in December 2001.

The process of ensuring quality is multifaceted. ISO 9001:2000 includes such things as design verification, process validation, process control and product testing. If some of these components are not properly deployed or are poorly executed, the quality of the output will suffer. It does not matter how well a product is made if it is the wrong product. The same is true for a good design that is poorly executed. That is why quality system implementation must go beyond mere satisfaction of audit criteria. An audit can determine whether a company has a procedure for design validation (say, for a new tire design) and can determine whether that procedure is being followed. However, a registration or surveillance audit cannot, in general, determine whether that procedure is the one that *ought* to be in place. The same goes for product and process testing (say, in a plant beset by a strike) or customer satisfaction data (say, regarding problems encountered in use). Beyond existence and compliance lies effectiveness.

CURRENT TRENDS IN CONSENSUS STANDARDS

Standards development is evolutionary. However, high-tech industries — especially where reliability and safety are prime requirements — have always recognized that their goal is not to achieve the "lowest common denominator" but to use the standards as a starting point from which to proceed toward excellence.

As a result, certain industries have added a sort of "ISO-plus" to the ISO standard industry-specific requirements to ensure that registered enterprises exceed that lowest common denominator. For example:

❖ Auto industry   ISO/TS 16949

❖ Telecommunications industry   TL 9000

❖ Aerospace industry   AS9100

Both TL 9000 and AS9100 are international consensus standards created by their respective industries. Many of the add-ons in these standards are not really peculiar to those industries, but represent practices that the industry wishes to normalize. For example, whereas ISO 9001 has always required that measurement certainty be known, automakers, who receive thousands of parts measured by hundreds of suppliers, require that suppliers use a common analytical method to reduce the variations in the type and quantity of data in part submissions.

ISO requires that standards be reviewed every five years to determine whether they should be updated, deleted or retained. ISO 9001:2000 is the third edition of the international quality standard, incorporating a subtle transformation from quality assurance to quality management. The member bodies of TC 176, viewing customer needs as the force behind the revision, identified four main reasons for change:

1. The need for a common structure similar to the Malcolm Baldrige National Quality Award criteria.

2. The need for continual improvement and prevention of nonconformity — a clear push toward performance measurement.

3. The need for ease of use and clarity of terminology (an attempt to harmonize the requirements of service and manufacturing industries).

4. The need for compatibility with ISO 14001, the environmental management system standard.

A major difference in the 2000 iteration of ISO 9001 is that the standard is organized along a process model. The earlier versions had been based on a build-to-contract model, which was not surprising since they were derived

FIGURE 2-4 PROCESS MODEL IMPLIED IN ISO 9001:1994

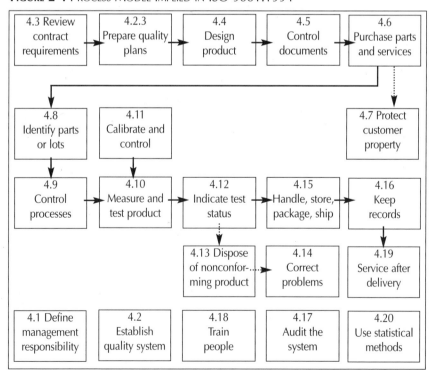

FIGURE 2-5 PROCESS MODEL USED IN ISO 9001:2000

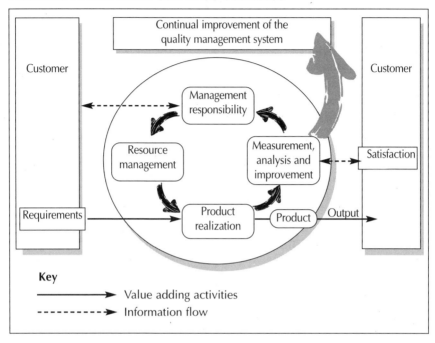

from MIL-Q-9858A (see Figure 2-4). In that model, we proceeded from tender (request for proposal) through contract, design and production, to service following installation. Once the end item was completely assembled for final test, it was disassembled (handled) and stored until the customer requested delivery and installation.

The requirements of both ISO 9001:2000 and ISO 9001:1994 are understood to extend to *all* handling, storage and so forth. Note that the requirements do not require on-time delivery, only assurance that quality will not be compromised by the delivery process. This is not an oversight. ISO 9001 is a quality management standard, not a logistics management standard. It is concerned with delivering an acceptable end item. Some industry-specific standards, such as ISO/TS 16949, set logistical requirements as well as quality requirements.

While some changes in ISO 9001:2000 definitely enhance the usefulness of the document, some are less helpful than others. "Production" has been replaced by "product realization." If the goal is to include service and transactional operations along with manufacturing, that goal has been achieved. However, the new term is equally opaque to everyone.

This old model was not especially applicable to other sorts of operations, for example "build to stock then market," or service and transactional businesses. Consequently, the new version employs a more general model that connects customer input to internal processes and uses customer satisfaction, confidence and feedback to recharge the business processes in a continuous improvement loop — the plan-do-study-act of total quality management, discussed in the next chapter. This is illustrated in Figure 2-5, which is taken from the ISO 9001:2000 standard.

Prior to the 2000 release, ISO 9000 was written in the style of MIL-Q-9858A, which was intended to be a contract requirement on a supplier. Thus, many sentences begin "The supplier shall...." This terminology confused some companies that were trying to implement the system and were not accustomed to the contractor model. The 2000 version replaces "supplier" with "organization." Our recommendation is that you replace "organization" with the name of your company and "product" with the name of your end item or deliverable. This often helps to clarify the requirements.

The most obvious difference in the new version is the numbering scheme. The familiar 20 elements of ISO 9001:1994 have been replaced with five major sections:

1. Quality Management System.

2. Management Responsibility.

3. Resource Management.

4. Product Realization.

5. Measurement, Analysis and Improvement.

What might not be apparent is that all of the previous 20 elements are alive and well in the new sections. (To assure users that continuity is maintained, Annex B of ISO 9001:2000 contains an element-by-element cross-reference to ISO 9001:1994.)

How does the new standard affect your operations?

1. The new version emphasizes strengthening the supply chain through organization-to-customer communication, written and unwritten specifications, contract and design/development review, process management and supplier and customer feedback.

2. The organization must determine measurement opportunities in all aspects of the business — order specification, training, process management, nonconformity monitoring and customer satisfaction — not just for the end item or deliverable. Also, it is not sufficient to merely

collect measurements. The organization must analyze the data for fact-based decision making as a means of achieving continual improvement.

3. The need to meet customer requirements is represented in every part of the business transaction, not solely in production/operations. Organizations must go·beyond "meeting specs" and be aware of and respond positively to "fitness for purpose," unspecified requirements, process efficiencies, mid-stream changes, postproduction activities and customer satisfaction. The standard refers to this process as achieving "customer confidence." This is tricky ground, as it is difficult to evaluate satisfaction with unspecified requirements.

Some organizations have suggested that the new standard will force them to rewrite much of their documentation, add new staff functions (statisticians, for example) and add activities to their already full agendas — all as required changes to an already ISO 9001-registered quality management system. If they do so, however, it would be their own decision based on their own analysis of the standard and may reflect the size and complexity of their business rather than the nature of the new requirements. It's true that more activities will be needed to support the new requirements, and some businesses will want to hire process engineers, customer advocates and data managers. Regarding additional documentation, it's estimated that an ISO 9001/2:1994-registered organization is at least 80 percent of the way to ISO 9001:2000 compliance. The main outward difference is a revised or reorganized quality manual and several new procedures; the purposes of these changes are to strengthen the continual improvement process. Meanwhile, the detailed work instructions people use to do their daily jobs are rarely affected.

In the final analysis, ISO 9001:2000 attempts to take a major step beyond traditional quality control and quality assurance systems to become a basic model for a modern, information-based, customer-driven quality management system that adds value to an organization's processes. As a standard written by a committee of more than 100 international experts, it contains compromises and apparent contradictions. If these are overcome, and if the standard is implemented with the purpose of improving customer satisfaction, ISO 9001:2000 and its industry-specific derivatives have the potential to become a worldwide model for the next generation of quality management systems. However, a quality management system is only that — a documented description of how an organization operates and a means for supplying objective evidence that it is operating that way. The system itself assures neither quality nor continual improvement, and a third-party auditor cannot readily determine anything except whether or not you have a system and are following it without a more in-depth audit focused on evaluating the efficacy of the system.

MOVING ON TO EXCELLENCE

You should now have a better orientation for the world of consensus standards and regulations. As discussed earlier, the latest versions of these standards and regulations emphasize continual improvement, process approach and customer satisfaction. These areas of interest are stepping-stones that should enable organizations to grow from ISO 9001:2000 to Six Sigma and performance excellence — all of which are elements of the Fusion Management process. Of the three components of Fusion Management — operations, tactics and strategy — we have examined the first: operations (see Figure 2-6).

Many executives have learned the hard way — too often as a result of product recalls or regulatory consent decrees — that constant attention to improving business, quality and regulatory processes is far less expensive and yields far greater returns on investment than most alternative approaches. It is certainly more productive than "benign neglect" or "bull of the woods" management systems. Leadership that fully commits to a business excellence model is far less likely to be on television apologizing for performance deficiencies.

"Excellence is what makes freedom ring and isn't that what we do best?" With those words, President Reagan challenged US companies during his January 1987 State of the Union address. Many in the United States supported Reagan's position, especially as it related to American businesses and foreign trade, but management must not allow itself to be lulled into thinking that Washington-inspired policies will make up for low levels of commitment in the boardroom. Worldwide, companies wage warfare in a battle to win export trade and expand domestic sales through excellence. To be competitive in today's

FIGURE 2-6 COMPONENTS OF FUSION MANAGEMENT

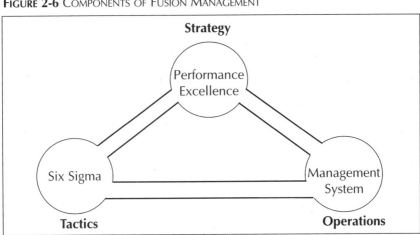

global marketplace, companies must achieve world-class quality and survive and prosper by going far beyond mandated levels of minimally acceptable quality.

An old equation states:

$$\textbf{Customer Satisfaction} = \frac{\textbf{Quality}}{\textbf{Cost}}$$

Here, "quality" is the totality of features that satisfy or delight the customer. Too often, management has concentrated on the denominator, slashing costs, often at the expense of quality. They are surprised when customers desert them. In fact, in many cases, they do not cut costs at all; they only spend less money, which is not the same. A printing house, for example, once tried to cut costs by using cheaper paper. But the cheaper paper did not have all the qualities of the more expensive product. Its tensile strength was less, so that breakage and scrap increased in the press room; and the surface finish was rougher. White specks due to "picking" appeared in the photographs. Since one of the magazines it printed was an astronomy journal, the sudden appearance of white specks was not a good thing. In the end, by spending less money, the printing business found that its costs had increased while revenues decreased.

The opposite mistake is just as bad. A computer firm's line of personal computers once failed and the president declared in a memo, "We tried to put too much quality [into the product]." By this he meant "too many features" that the prospective customers did not demand. A quality engineer in a can plant was accused of wanting "a gold-plated beer can." But gold plating was not a quality desired by the customer. Had any can been somehow gold-plated, it would have been a defect.

To meet tough international competition, businesses that wish to export to expand their markets and nations that want to improve their trade balances must work to implement comprehensive processes to achieve excellence. This objective requires more than quick fixes. It requires that management and employees work together to achieve higher levels of excellence.

During the late 1970s, American management began listening to some of the world's quality leaders — Crosby, Deming, Ishikawa and Juran, among others. However, a root problem in the United States is that American business schools do not rigorously instill a comprehensive, information-driven approach to the quality process. In his address, President Reagan observed, "The quest for excellence into the 21st century begins in the school but must go next to the workplace." In the next two chapters, we will look at quality-driven initiatives that go beyond ISO 9001:2000 to provide the tools and measures — the dynamics and direction — that ISO 9001 hints at.

3
Improving What We Do

"Improvement" is a term with many fans but few coaches. Everyone is in favor of it, but no one seems quite sure how to go about it. Many management programs have a series of steps, and one of these invariably is "solve the problem." It's hard to argue with this advice, but it's also hard to carry it out. If the first element to be *fused* is a management structure that enables an organization to achieve good results "on purpose," the second element is an engine that drives that organization forward to an excellence built on continual improvement.

There has seldom been any difficulty in solving certain problems. But "low-hanging fruit" does not really constitute a problem. Typically, this phrase refers to situations for which causes are self-evident or solutions already known. The only piece missing is the organizational will to actually do something. Then along comes the latest *programme du jour*. The troops are mobilized under this new banner, and the fruit is plucked. At that point, everything grinds to a halt because no one is quite sure how to reach the fruit on the higher branches.

We need a ladder.

Actually, we need more than that, because — to build on the metaphor — we also need to know whether to plant additional fruit trees or, indeed, whether we should be growing fruit at all. In other words, there is more to continual improvement than solving the problems of existing processes. There is no sense in improving operations for a product or service that no one wants. That's why continual improvement must be fused with strategic planning. Otherwise, we wind up solving the wrong problems.

EFFECTIVENESS AND EFFICIENCY

There are two aspects to improvement. One focuses on improving the qualities (features) of the output — we call this "effectiveness." The other stresses providing the output in less time with fewer resources — we call this "efficiency." The first traces its ancestry from early attempts to apply statistical concepts through SQC and SPC to TQM and Six Sigma. The second has its origins in the time and motion studies of the Gilbreths and has been reincarnated variously as Kanban, Just-In-Time, Kaizen and Lean Enterprise.

The two aspects are complementary, of course. One reason for inefficiency is the need to replace, repair or rework defects and errors; efforts to reduce errors almost always result in less material usage and shorter cycle times. However, even when a process is producing acceptable output, there may still be opportunities to improve it.

Consider the following example.

Aluminum cans have an interior coating that acts as a barrier between the metal and the contents of the can. If the can contains beer, the coating protects the beer from acquiring a "tinny" taste. If it contains soda, the coating protects the aluminum from being corroded by the soda. One of the qualities of the can, therefore, is its *film weight*. If this is too low, pinholes (or even thin spots) will allow the migration of ions or the leaking of material through the coating layer. Actually, coating thickness is the desired property, but this is not easily measured on the line. However, since gross weight and thickness correlate, one can be tracked as a surrogate for the other. This is an example of the choice of a *feasible metric*.

If it is too high, we will add cost without adding value.

Coating weight had such wide variation that the target value was set many milligrams above the minimum needed to ensure continuity and adequate thickness. Investigations using statistical analyses identified the major cause of the variation to be test procedure. In a misguided attempt to save money, test cans were reused. This approach resulted in artificially high readings on the second sample of each shift, which in turn motivated the operator to over-adjust the spray guns.

After the procedure was changed, the operator made 70 percent fewer adjustments and the variation shrank by 50 percent. The process was, in fact, so stable that the second sample on each shift was dropped, which meant 50 percent fewer inspections. Finally, the target value was lowered by several milligrams because, given the reduced variation, there was little risk of individual cans falling below the critical weight. The total savings in material costs alone were estimated in excess of $1 million per year.

This same company was also experimenting with different coatings in anticipation of emission standards being tightened. Together, these examples illustrate two aspects of continual output improvement: namely, achieving a breakthrough on the status quo of an existing operation and anticipating and planning for a potential future problem.

EVERYTHING WE NEED TO KNOW ABOUT QUALITY WAS PUBLISHED BY 1931!

In the foreword, I stated somewhat facetiously that everything we need to know about quality dates back to 1931, when Dr. Walter Shewhart's book, *Economic Control of Quality of Manufactured Product*, was first published.

Although language and terminology have shifted somewhat since then, it is startling to realize how up-to-date Shewhart's book is. It may lack the catchy titles favored by the postmodern era, but it is easy to see what so impressed W. Edwards Deming that he spent years learning at the feet of this man.

The book emphasizes focusing on the customer ("translating wants into physical characteristics") and minimizing process variation, both major components of today's Six Sigma philosophy. Simply put, all variation costs money. Consider the thickness of the chrome plating on a surgical scalpel. The thicker it gets, the more the material cost per unit goes up. But as it gets thinner, pinholes may open up, resulting in corrosion and costs due to failure and possible claims. The optimum amount of chrome is just enough to avoid pinholes, but no more. Any variation from that optimum, even within tolerances, will cost money.

Every process has some degree of random variation built into it. This "normal variation" is generally taken to be plus or minus three standard deviations. In statistical theory, this accounts for 99.73 percent of the items produced. (In practice, no real-world process is exactly like a statistical distribution.) Reducing variation means shrinking the standard deviation so that this normal variation is as small as possible. A "three sigma" performance level means that the process variation of ± 3 sigma exactly fits within the tolerance limits. In theory, this means that 0.27 percent of the items will be defective (or 2,700 defects per million opportunities), *provided the arithmetic mean (average) remains centered.*

Very few processes will remain centered indefinitely. Statistical techniques are good, but may not detect a small process change immediately. During this "stealth" phase (after the problem occurs, but before it is detected), some larger percentage of the output will be unacceptable. The largest such process change that might go undetected for a short time is a shift in the mean of 1.5 standard deviations from the target. During this time, the error rate will jump to 66,810 defects per million opportunities (DPMO).

If the variation is reduced so that the tolerance limits lie farther away from the mean, a disturbance to the process will not have such a drastic effect. If sigma is so small that the tolerances lay at a distance of six sigma, then a process disturbance of 1.5 sigma will result in only 3.4 DPMO until the problem is discovered and corrected. Since the process is unlikely to produce millions of units during this time (some transactional processes excepted), it is unlikely that any rejections will need to be dealt with.

Shewhart's approach to process capability was to control the aim and minimize variation of the process and therefore the product. Most well-run organizations are running closer to four sigma (6,210 DPMO peak). Hence, there is still plenty of room for continual improvement and breakthrough efforts.

Going back to 1931, it is clear that much of what we talk about today concerning approaches to process improvement was discussed then.

- ❖ Shewhart focused on understanding customer wants and designing to satisfy those wants.
- ❖ Shewhart used "control charts" to identify shifts in the mean (average), the variation and to identify improvement opportunities.
- ❖ Sir Ronald A. Fisher and others developed concepts of design of experiments in agriculture and chemical industry.
- ❖ Frank and Lillian Gilbreth were using "time and motion studies" to reduce cycle time.

This concept of economic control of quality laid the foundation for quality management as we know it today. Unfortunately, those organizations that tried to implement Shewhart's concepts of process capability studies and process control often did not fully understand them and applied them mechanically; hence, results were often not what they should have been.

SOME BACKGROUND ON CONTINUAL IMPROVEMENT

A number of elements must be fused for continual improvement to work well. These include statistical methods of analysis, planning, human factors and process efficiency methods.

Past initiatives have missed this point and have emphasized one facet at the expense of others. We have been told that we would improve, if we worked in teams, or hourly people worked in groups, or we plotted control charts, or we designed experiments and so on (Figure 3-1). Often, these approaches were presented as alternatives. Some practitioners played down the motivational aspects of Crosby's Zero Defects ("mere hoopla") and then tried to implement their own improvements without the motivation and hoopla — they soon found how far a lack of enthusiasm would take them. The Marines did not go ashore

FIGURE 3-1 EVOLUTION OF SIX SIGMA

❖ Acceptance Sampling...1920s
❖ Control Charts...1920s
❖ Hawthorne Studies..1930s
❖ Design of Experiments...1930s
❖ Statistical Quality Control..1940s
❖ Management by Objectives..1950s
❖ Zero Defects...1960s
❖ Participative Problem Solving...1970s
❖ Quality Circles..1970s
❖ Total Quality Control/Companywide Quality Control....................1970s
❖ Statistical Process Control...1970s
❖ Kaizen...1970s
❖ Total Quality Management..1980s
❖ Quality Gurus...1980s
❖ Statistically Aided Management™*...1980s
❖ Lean Enterprise...1980s
❖ Baldrige Award...1980s
❖ Six Sigma...1990s
* Statistically Aided Management is a trademark of STAT-A-MATRIX, Inc.

on Iwo Jima just because it made logical sense or because there was a well-thought-out strategic plan (although it did and there was); but neither did they go ashore solely because of the motivation and patriotic "hoopla."

ACCEPTANCE SAMPLING

During the 1920s researchers centered at Bell Telephone Laboratories and Western Electric began to apply statistical methods to quality control. Foremost among them were Shewhart, who first described the control chart in a memo dated May 16, 1924 (and who taught both Juran and Deming), and Dodge and Romig, who jointly developed acceptance-sampling plans that used inspection data for control.

Although Unit Tolerances have been with us since the early 1800s, the concept of Lot Tolerance is more recent. When the era of mass production bloomed in the early 1900s, inspectors were faced with the problem of evaluating large quantities of items. There were far too many to inspect each one, even with the go/no-go gauges developed for this purpose. The practice arose of inspecting a few items from each "lot" and accepting or rejecting the lot depending on the sample results.

The results were mixed.

Clearly, the approach reduced the inspection workload, but also resulted in rejecting lots that had very few defectives and passing lots that had many. The cause was rooted in the practice of inspecting a "percentage sample."

A percentage sample considers a fixed percentage of a lot, say 10 percent. Each lot of 100 pieces would have 10 pieces pulled, while a lot of 1,000 pieces would have a sample of 100 pieces pulled. This approach resulted, although people did not know it, in very loose acceptance criteria for small lots and very tight criteria for large lots because the ability of a sample to detect a stated lot quality is almost independent of the size of the lot.

Dodge and Romig defined "lot quality" as an analog to "unit quality." In place of a tolerance on each unit, they proposed a Lot Tolerance Percent Defective (LTPD) and designed sampling plans to ensure the likely rejection of lots outside this tolerance. Implicit in these plans were "nominal" values or acceptable quality levels (AQLs). When confronted with a lot, the inspector must decide whether to screen the lot beforehand or to allow the defectives to be discovered as the lot is used. The latter is more expensive per defective unit found, but if the number of such units is small, it will cost less than inspecting every unit in the lot. The AQL was intended to be the point below which discovery in use was less expensive than prior screening. This concept, as we have seen, was widely misunderstood afterward to mean that "some defectives were acceptable."

THE HUMAN FACTOR: HAWTHORNE STUDIES

The Hawthorne Studies were performed by Professor Elton Mayo of the Harvard Business School at the Western Electric Hawthorne Works in Chicago, Illinois, from 1927 to 1932. The studies were a follow-up to a series of experiments performed at the plant between 1924 and 1927. These earlier experiments had failed to find a clear relationship between the level of illumination in the work place and productivity. The studies involved selecting a group of employees to help management improve performance. The group was set aside from the regular assembly lines in an area where the light intensity (illumination) could be controlled. A supervisor was put in the room with the assemblers to help them, not discipline them.

The study started with the ambient lighting at the standard level, and productivity was recorded. The lighting intensity was raised and productivity went up. The illumination was raised again, and productivity continued to go up. Management was convinced that they had found a cause-and-effect relationship between illumination and productivity. To validate these results, they decided to reduce the illumination, fully expecting the productivity to go down. But each time they lowered the light intensity, the productivity either rose or stayed the same. In total frustration, they ended their studies and then retained Elton Mayo.

Mayo's findings were contrary to the existing theory that workers were motivated solely by economic interests. Mayo realized, for example, that the women in the experiment had formed a social relationship that included the supervisor. They were happier at work than their co-workers on the shop floor and they had higher self-esteem. Instead of being called "Operator 6," they were called by their names. They felt part of a team, and they would do whatever it took to keep productivity high.

This phenomenon became known as the Hawthorne Effect, and it demonstrated that the human element has to be considered in any process improvement design. Although this discovery of an *esprit de corps* was not new, no one had thought to apply it to a work group. It has become such a truism today that we forget it had to be discovered. Even today, there are managers who know it but fail to behave as if it were true.

Unmotivated and alienated workers cannot produce continual improve-ment, but the converse is not true. That is, a motivated and engaged work force is necessary, but cannot alone achieve continual improvement. To produce con-tinual improvement, we need to *fuse* motivation with methods.

WORLD WAR II AND THE PUSH FOR QUALITY

In the 1940s, members of the Western Electric team and others were brought together by the US War Department (now the Department of Defense) to develop statistical methods to enhance the quality of products for the war effort. This group met at Columbia University (later they were referred to as the Columbia Research Group) to come up with ways to improve quality and productivity. They created military standards for sampling, such as MIL-STD-105 (for inspection by attributes) and MIL-STD-414 (for inspection by vari-ables for percent defective). These documents were designed to make scientif-ic sampling easier to apply by government contractors.

The War Department had difficulty getting manufacturers to agree to acceptance sampling. Manufacturers were concerned that the military would take a small sample and find "only" one or two defects in a lot (or batch) and reject the entire lot. Rejection could mean 100 percent inspection of the remaining parts; scrapping, reworking or reprocessing the defective parts; and/or withholding payment. The manufacturers were concerned about Type I errors — the rejection of acceptable lots. "Acceptable" meant containing few enough defects that discovery in use was more economical than additional screening. (The legal equivalent is convicting an innocent person on circum-stantial evidence.) Common phrases for this type of error are *Crying Wolf, Wild Goose Chase* and *False Alarm*.

The Dodge-Romig tables were based on LTPD — in essence, it was an assurance that lots with a percent of defectives greater than the LTPD would be rejected. The military, as customer, was concerned with the possibility that too many "duds" would be accepted. This is a Type II error. Common phrases for this are *Asleep at the Switch* and *Fat, Dumb and Happy*.

Every sample has a tendency to overestimate or underestimate the true quality of the lot, so there is a certain risk of Type I and Type II errors for any given AQL and LTPD. Consider the accompanying diagram (Figure 3-2). It shows how a sample size of n = 100 will operate when the acceptance rule is to accept if c ≤ 2 defectives (less than or equal to two errors or defects per 100).

FIGURE 3-2 OPERATING CHARACTERISTIC CURVE (OCC)

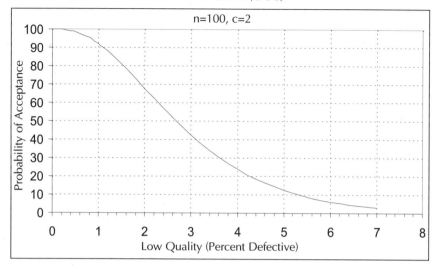

If the lots presented for inspection contain 1 percent errors or less, the probability of rejecting these lots and screening them unnecessarily would be about 10 percent or less. Conversely, if the lots are as bad as 5 percent errors or more, the sampling plan will accept them only about 10 percent of the time or less. On the other hand, when the lot quality is around 2.6 percent, the sampling plan will accept them about half the time. This is like tossing a coin to decide whether to accept a lot or not — only first you inspect 100 pieces!

Note that if a series of lots is presented, all of exactly the same quality, some will be accepted and some will be rejected. The proportion of each will depend on the lot quality. The rejected lots will not be any worse than the accepted lots and vice versa. If all lots were essentially alike, there would be no need to perform an acceptance sample to decide whether screening was needed. We would know from the process average whether all lots could be used as-is or had to be screened before use. Only when the individual lot quality was uncertain would a sample be required to aid in the decision.

ECONOMIC CONTROL OF QUALITY OF MANUFACTURED PRODUCT

What was needed was a tool that would determine whether each lot in a series of lots was consistently of the same quality to indicate whether any particular segment was in need of special treatment. Fortunately, such a tool already existed in the form of Shewhart's control chart.

If a series of lots (or samples from a process) remains between statistically calculated limits, the lots can be regarded as essentially alike in quality and can be handled or treated in the same way. Shewhart called this "a state of statistical control." Today, we say "in control," but the phrase refers only to the consistency of the quality, not to whether that quality is acceptable.

However, Shewhart had more in mind than improving acceptance sampling by adding the concept of a "grand lot" of mutually consistent lots. He created the concept of a *capability study*. This meant a persistent search for causes of variation with the aim of eliminating or controlling them in order to reduce variation to the process' minimum. Unfortunately, for many people today, a capability study is simply a menu item on a software package, an essentially static analysis. It is a way of measuring the current capability and recording it, rather than a dynamic process for reducing variation and controlling the aim of the process.

Even today, many suppliers (who are required by their customers to use control charts and to post the charts near the processes being monitored) misapply the technique. We frequently visit companies that proudly show us their control charts. When we ask what actions are taken when points exceed control limits, managers typically respond, "We don't take any action; we don't know what to do," or, "Nothing is ever outside the limits."

In one case, a manufacturer of computer circuit boards had an entire wall of control charts. All of them were badly out of control. None of them had generated any action. The response was, "We just plot these because the customer wants us to."

In another case, a manufacturer of glass windshields plotted charts of the thickness measured at five locations as part of a customer's requirement. "The charts don't help us," they said. "They're always in control, and we know the process is out of control." They were asked how they knew. "There is a sixth location that really tells us what's happening." When asked why they don't plot a chart of that location, the response was, "Are you crazy? It would be out of control and the customer (who received copies of all the charts) would be upset."

A statistician at a financial institution was engaged in a similar search for metrics that never went out of control. Her customer required copies of all charts and had a rule that "95 percent of the charts for a given month must be in control." By including a large number of "good but useless" charts she could satisfy the customer and then concentrate on the smaller number of "bad but useful" charts that contained clues to continual improvement.

My last example is a packaging company that produced very large laminated cardboard boxes. They kept charts recording deviations of more than plus or minus a quarter-of-an inch in box height. They went years without exceeding their control limits, collecting mountains of data that were never used and had nothing to do with improving their processes. These types of control charts are, of course, non-value-added and should either be abolished or used properly. The purpose of control charting is to identify causes of abnormal behavior, not to produce pretty wallpaper. Remember: the key word is *control*, not *chart*.

Many companies fail to realize that charts that are always in control are not especially useful for improvement. Only by identifying an abnormal behavior can we identify and correct its causes. By the way, this statement applies to abnormally *good* behavior as well. Some organizations fail to put control limits on the positive side of certain processes. Consider a bank that plots the number of days it takes to clear a check. Typically, they will take action when the process seems out of control on the negative side. But what about "out-of-control" positive results? If we can investigate why we are accidentally getting better-than-expected results, we can perhaps institute the controls needed to stay better on purpose permanently.

ANOTHER PERSPECTIVE

We once worked with a client running a high-volume fill operation. We had coached them in doing process capability studies, and a few project teams had performed these studies on processes with major improvement opportunities. At a meeting with the plant's senior executive team, the project teams reported that the studies completed to date would yield a $7 million cost reduction over the next 12 months. The general manager and many of his direct reports seemed hesitant. I requested a break and met with the general manager outside the meeting room. Eventually he commented, "Can you imagine how the New York office would react if they learned that we have been throwing away $7 million a year?" We discussed the report further and agreed to report the estimated cost savings as $3 million. At the end of the following year the actual savings were reported as $8 million: $3 million "as a result of process capability studies" and $5 million due to "nonspecified initiatives."

Dr. Deming expressed the need to "drive out fear." In this case, we failed to do that. Imagine a general manager afraid to report a significant improvement! Imagine a head office that would react to improvement with hostility and accusations! But over the following two years, we did work with the New York office to help them understand how endemic fear was in their organization. We helped them recognize and address the policies, both stated and unstated, that contributed to that fear.

Plot the Data

Dr. Ellis R. Ott was a mathematics professor at Rutgers University who developed a Department of Applied Statistics and Quality Control, offering M.S. and Ph.D. degrees. Between the 1950s and the 1970s, hundreds of full-time professionals were educated by Dr. Ott and a prestigious group of faculty members. Dr. Ott would always tell his students to collect data, but always reminded them to "plot the data" before trying to analyze it. Most people are amazed at how frequently data speaks to them. A great deal of success in problem solving can be attributed to the technique of choosing various alternative graphic plots of data. Ellis Ott retired from Rutgers University in 1972 to join the STAT-A-MATRIX staff, and he has since trained hundreds of professionals around the world.

Statistical Quality Control

This topic has had as many lives as a cat! Statistical Quality Control (SQC) was used by some organizations in the 1920s and 1930s and, during World War II, as we have noted, it received a lot of attention. When the war was over and commercial goods were again in demand, SQC was set aside, except by the military and, later, NASA. For a time, it did not matter if a product was good or bad; the pent-up demand was so great that anything could be sold. Mediocre quality and built-in obsolescence became a way of life in an era when people planned to trade in cars every three years. The absence of customer complaints, however, did not mean customers were satisfied.

After the gasoline shortages of the 1970s, for example, many consumers in the United States began to equate automotive quality with fuel economy and switched to the more fuel-efficient foreign imports. However, when they realized that the imports were more reliable than Detroit's offerings, lacking the built-in obsolescence to which they had become accustomed and including many "standard" rather than "extra" innovative engineering features, many consumers remained loyal to the imports — even when they moved up to luxury models.

Even in the 1940s, people recognized the need for applying SQC to commercial products. The following quote is from the First Annual Convention of the American Society for Quality Control, June 5 and 6, 1947, in Chicago, Illinois. The luncheon address was given by C.R. Sheaffer, president of the W.A. Sheaffer Pen Co., and the topic was "What Top Management Expects from Quality Control."

> "The advent of new precision, engineered, quality products with their extremely close tolerances, compared to pre-war standards, demands that we all become increasingly quality-minded. It is imperative that we must now concern ourselves as never before with increasing quality, because we know that as competition becomes more keen, the ability to win and hold a market will constantly bring into focus the importance of producing a quality product which will justify acceptance by the consumer. The consuming public is becoming more critical both in price and quality, and it has a perfect right to become critical. Thus, we must make use of this newest management tool, quality control, to insure maintenance of top quality, at lowest cost."

Most readers will agree that, with just a few changes, this paragraph could have come out of a contemporary speech on what top management expects. Sheaffer also said in his speech, "We believe [my father] made an indelible impression upon our organization regarding the policy Quality First, and he has left a heritage to follow." Most readers will recognize "Quality First" as a typical summary of corporate policy coming from contemporary top managers.

Although application in the 1950s was sporadic, SQC reemerged in the early 1960s when efforts were made to use it more effectively. By the late 1960s, however, Management by Objectives and Zero Defects were the reigning fads, and SQC was put on the back burner once again. The early 1970s brought quality circles and the application of some basic problem solving and SQC tools. This was followed by another reemergence of SQC under the new name of Statistical Process Control (SPC). The 1980s and 1990s brought Total Quality Management (TQM) and Six Sigma, both of which emphasized quantitative analytical tools. Particularly in the automotive industry, TQM was used to get US quality up to the level of the foreign imports. So far, this cat has used six or seven lives.

Total Quality Control (from the United States to Japan)

Professor Kaoru Ishikawa and the Japanese Union of Scientists and Engineers (JUSE) led Japan's drive to improve the quality of its products. JUSE was formed in 1946, and in 1949 JUSE established the Quality Control Research Group (QCRG), whose purpose was to engage in research and the dissemination of knowledge in quality control. Its goal was to raise the living standard in Japan by improving the quality of its products. The intent was to create favorable trade balances and Japanese prosperity.

The QCRG conducted its first basic quality control course in September 1949, which was held three days each month for a year. After that, the ongoing program involved six days of training per month for six months. The original courses employed British and American standards translated into Japanese. Later courses, which used texts prepared by the QCRG, focused on Japanese culture and taught statistical quality control, which became popular in Japan in the 1950s.

After World War II, Bell Telephone technicians working with their Japanese counterparts explained the usefulness of Shewhart's charts. JUSE invited Shewhart to come to Japan and lecture on quality control. But "the Master" was ill — he would die a few years later — and he suggested that they invite his protégé, W. Edwards Deming. A statistician who had worked for the US Census Bureau among other clients, Deming was familiar with Shewhart's work and had spent time studying under him. Later, he would edit and publish

Figure 3-3 Shewhart Cycle

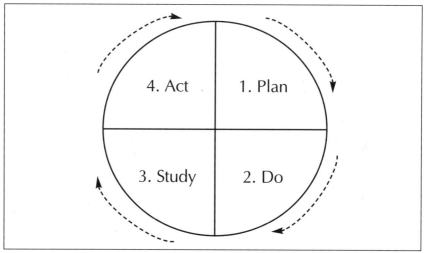

a series of Shewhart's lectures. It was Deming who always referred to Shewhart as "the Master."

Deming brought to Japan the concepts of "statistical thinking" that were developed at Bell Telephone Laboratories. In 1950, Deming hosted an eight-day seminar on statistical quality control for managers and engineers. In addition, he offered a special one-day seminar to company presidents and top managers in Hakone, Japan. He believed that such a seminar would lead senior executives to comprehend the importance of quality control for their companies and country. Although Ishikawa and others had been doing similar work, it was Deming's lectures that were the springboard for the Japanese recovery. As one American observer said later, "The Japanese thought we were actually doing all that." Deming himself remarked on his failure to motivate American executives during the postwar period, "It's hard to convince a man who is making money that he is doing it wrong."

Deming returned to Japan in 1951 and 1952 to provide a follow-up and introduced the "Shewhart Cycle" of plan-do-study-act (PDSA) (Figure 3-3). This became a very important paradigm or strategy for Japan and later for much of the world. During his lifetime Deming returned to Japan frequently.

As a result of Deming's lectures and classes, engineers and workers in Japan practiced quality control, but top and middle managers still did not show much interest. To fill this void, JUSE invited Joseph Juran to visit Japan in 1954. He conducted seminars for senior executives, explaining their roles and responsibilities in promoting quality control. Juran's visit created an atmosphere that stressed quality control as a management tool, resulting in what the Japanese referred to afterward as *total quality control*.

In 1951, JUSE created the Deming Prize to encourage Japanese companies to improve the quality of their products. The Deming Prize is given annually to major corporations who win a rigorous quality-control competition. Deming had provided statistical thinking and tools for improvement, and Juran added a managerial approach to deploying such tools (Breakthrough Management). The Deming Prize brought it all together. Managers, supervisors and technical people focused on projects to improve their processes and products.

Japanese visits to the United States in the 1960s led the Japanese to develop their own approaches to American methods and tools. In many respects, the Japanese listened to what we said we were doing and elected to follow many of our approaches. Unfortunately, we were talking the talk, but not walking the walk. The 1970s were Japan's years of total quality control, or *companywide quality control*. We provided the Japanese with tools that were available to us, but which we did not use ourselves.

By the late 1970s, many American companies complained that the Japanese were "dumping product" in the United States; that is, we claimed that they were selling products below cost in order to capture the market. We reached this conclusion because we could not make the product for what they were charging in the United States, let alone the cost to ship it from Japan. Some years later we realized that the Japanese were indeed able to make a profit — by using the very tools that we had shown them. The Japanese were also accused of using "unfair, nontariff barriers to American goods." (A business magazine at the time printed a list of these unfair barriers; most of them were quality specifications.) As the British magazine, *The Economist*, noted after Lee Iacocca's trip to Japan, "What Mr. Iacocca forgot to mention was that Chrysler makes minivans with the steering wheel on the wrong side."

In fact, during this period, Japanese buyers were the second largest group of customers for US exports, after Canada. On a per capita basis, the average Japanese spent slightly more on American-made goods than the average American spent on Japanese-made goods. The trade balance was unfavorable because there were only half as many Japanese as there were Americans, and they had about the same amount of money in their pockets.

The real question was not why Japan bought half as much, but how a country its size *produced* so much. Partly, this was the result of government policies that encouraged exports and focused efforts on designated products and industries. (Japan has virtually no natural resources and must import nearly all the iron, coal and other raw materials it needs.) Japanese companies prospered because they had products to sell that were worth buying. Toyota entered the American automobile market *against* the advice of the Ministry of International Trade and Industry (MITI), the government agency that supposedly orchestrated the Japanese economy.

While managers and technical people focused on high priority projects (the "vital few"), many smaller opportunities were not being addressed. Individually, these "useful many" did not have a high return on investment. They were not worth the time of the managers and technical people. Collectively, however, they were still a tidy opportunity. If operations-level people tackled them, the return on investment (ROI) problem would not be so acute. This realization led, as we have seen, to the creation of QC or quality circles, in which operational personnel used the PDSA approach to solve problems. The first of these circles arose spontaneously, and some Japanese practitioners have said that the circles achieved their best results *before* QC circles were made into a formal program.

The Japanese used the terms total quality control, companywide quality control and QC circles to describe their approaches. Ironically, as we have seen, the Japanese first succeeded by mimicking what they believed the United States to be doing in terms of applying statistical thinking, managerial breakthrough and other approaches and tools. The Japanese, however, did adapt and augment these American ideas. They built specific tools and approaches such as Just-In-Time (JIT), Single Minute Exchange of Die (SMED), Kaizen and Lean Manufacturing — ideas that we have, in turn, borrowed from Japan.

The Japanese considered worker education in quality control very important, but initially found it very difficult to achieve. Japan's massive work force, scattered across the entire country, couldn't be gathered together as easily as the country's engineers and staff personnel. The problem went unsolved until 1956, when a quality control correspondence course was broadcast to foremen through the Japan Shortwave Broadcasting Corporation. The following year, Japan Broadcasting Corporation (NHK) broadcast quality control educational programs and sold 110,000 copies of the text that accompanied the program. To follow up, JUSE published *A Text on Quality Control for Foremen*, which also sold very well.

Ishikawa emphasized the following attributes of QC circles.

1. **Volunteerism** — Circles are to be created on a voluntary basis and not by a command from above. Begin circle activities with those people who wish to participate.

2. **Self-development** — Members must be willing to study.

3. **Mutual development** — Members must aspire to expand their horizons and cooperate with other circles.

4. **Eventual total participation** — Circles must establish as their ultimate goal the full participation of all workers in the workplace.

He cautioned that this approach may limit the initial growth of quality circles, but he felt that the Japanese QC circles prospered in the long run because of it.

FROM JAPAN BACK TO THE WEST

Ishikawa traveled throughout Western Europe and the United States, encouraging the growth of quality circles outside of Japan. JUSE also sent many missions to the United States, including groups of managers and quality circle teams visiting companies, universities and regional quality associations. From 1962 on, I had many opportunities to meet with these missions to share experiences. This approach led groups of American executives, in the 1970s and 1980s, to travel to Japan to witness what the Japanese were doing in terms of surpassing US quality. During these visits, American executives learned about the activities of Ishikawa, Juran and Deming in Japan, as well as the roles of upper and middle management and foremen in making improvements. However, what struck them most was the work of the quality circles — operator teams making improvements. For many American executives, this was an "aha!" experience. It encouraged them to conclude — mistakenly, as we have seen — that all they needed to do was to create quality circles at the operator level.

On a personal note, I founded the consulting firm STAT-A-MATRIX in 1968. Soon after, I joined forces with another consultant, Sidney Rubinstein, to work on a quality circle project that we called "participative problem solving." He had just returned from Japan and had some creative ideas on how to use the Japanese approaches, together with some unique approaches of his own. During the previous six years, I had been involved with teams of Japanese executives who were visiting the United States both to study what we were doing here and to make presentations on what they were doing there. As a result, participative problem solving evolved as a model that, first, integrated both Japanese and American approaches; second, incorporated qualitative, quantitative and behavioral change tools; and third, stressed differing approaches for senior executives, middle managers and operators. In 1970 and 1971, we arranged the first international conferences on quality circles in the United States, involving teams of Japanese and American companies sharing their experiences. Participative problem solving became accepted by a number of labor unions as a labor/management approach to improving business. The process had significant success in improving employee morale and using human resources and problem-solving tools to improve business processes.

TOTAL QUALITY MANAGEMENT

In 1979, NBC aired a program titled, "If Japan Can, Why Can't We?" This program featured Dr. W. Edwards Deming and emphasized how the Japanese had adopted Dr. Deming's ideas on statistical thinking. As a result of this program, many Americans wanted to emulate the Japanese, but they did not like the Japanese terms "Total Quality Control" and "Companywide Quality Control" because of the word "control," which seemed to have an authoritarian ring. Instead, Americans focused on "Total Quality Management" (TQM). A number of TQM "gurus" entered the scene, each with his own claim as to what TQM was.

Figure 3-4 is a matrix comparison of three of the more prominent gurus (Crosby, Deming and Juran) and a Fusion Management-oriented perspective.

FIGURE **3-4** COMPARISON OF TQM APPROACHES AND FUSION MANAGEMENT

Definition of Quality

Crosby	Juran
Conformance to requirements.	Fitness for use of products. Conformance to requirements for individuals.
Deming	**Fusion Management**
The customer determines what quality is.	Exceeding customer expectations.

Cost of Quality (COQ)

Crosby	Juran
COQ is a useful management tool. Consists of price of nonconformance and price of conformance. "Quality is free."	Quality of design costs but is repaid in the long run. Strive to remove chronic waste.
Deming	**Fusion Management**
COQ is not useful since elements of it are unknown and unknowable. Must minimize total cost.	Bottom-line business results are the true measure.

Statistical Quality Control (SQC)

Crosby	Juran
Recognizes usefulness in certain applications. Does not emphasize.	Discusses concepts.
Deming	**Fusion Management**
Study of variation is essential for sustained improvement. SQC used to avoid tampering while trying to improve.	Variation is the enemy!

Motivation

Crosby	Juran
Downplays motivation because of limited short-term value. Wants to achieve cultural change beginning with top management but involving everyone.	Necessary but not enough to solve problems.
Deming	**Fusion Management**
Create environment that fosters intrinsic motivation.	Involvement in teams and ownership of process and process improvement opportunities create an environment that motivates.

Figure 3-4 Continued

Acceptable Quality Level (AQL)

Crosby
Zero defects should always be sought. No AQLs.

Juran
Establish process capability during planning. Prove capability before implementation.

Deming
AQLs guarantee a level of nonconformance. Continual improvement is a must.

Fusion Management
Six Sigma targets make AQL obsolete.

Leadership Involvement

Crosby
Management commitment is first necessary step and must be continually maintained.

Juran
Success can't be achieved without it.

Deming
Leaders must know the work they supervise. Remove barriers. Operate consistent with profound knowledge.

Fusion Management
Senior executive team must be the leadership council that drives the process and serves as champions and mentors.

Vendor/Supplier Commitment

Crosby
Supplier/customer relationship viewed as vital part of requirements definition to ensure delivery of quality products.

Juran
Emphasis on supplier development. Strengthen customer/supplier relationship.

Deming
Need to build long-term loyalty and trust. End practice of awarding business on basis of price.

Fusion Management
Supplier partnerships that integrate the suppliers' process and customers' process into a single process.

Teamwork

Crosby
Quality improvement teams are driving force for planning. Corrective action teams also advocated.

Juran
Several programs designed for teams.

Deming
Used to implement the plan-do-study-act cycle. Everyone can participate to improve quality at each stage.

Fusion Management
Emphasis on full-time team leaders (black belts/master black belts) and part-time team members (green belts) with champions at executive level.

FIGURE 3-4 CONTINUED

Employee Involvement	
Crosby Strong emphasis on getting people to participate in all phases.	**Juran** Must make use of worker creativity by soliciting worker ideas on job-related activities.
Deming Employees encouraged to achieve pride of workmanship and take part in system improvement.	**Fusion Management** All employees will eventually participate in team activities as green or black belts.

Training and Education	
Crosby Education at all levels required so each can fulfill their role.	**Juran** Strong emphasis on providing skills for all levels and also leadership training.
Deming Institute vigorous program of education and self-improvement. Train people for the job.	**Fusion Management** Executive awareness. Executive champions/mentors. Master black belts, black belts, green belts.

Improvement Goals	
Crosby Goal setting is step in journey to zero defects.	**Juran** Strong emphasis on annual improvement goals.
Deming Downplays use of numerical goals and quotas. Also against MBO.	**Fusion Management** 10x improvement.

Recognition/Rewards	
Crosby Nonmonetary recognition is valid.	**Juran** Increased job satisfaction is form of reward.
Deming People require more than money. Restore joy of work. Eliminate performance evaluations and merit system.	**Fusion Management** The best one can expect to achieve is neutrality.

LEAN ENTERPRISE — A STEP TOWARD FUSION

Before moving on to Six Sigma, we need to at least briefly touch on another popular approach to improvement tools known as "Lean." Originally called "Lean Manufacturing," the process stems from the Toyota Production System (TPS) — an amalgam of methodologies including industrial engineering, Just-

In-Time (JIT), 5 S's, Total Quality Control (TQC), Continuous Quality Improvement (CQI), Visual Control, Total Productive Maintenance (TPM), Quality Circles and Kaizen. More recently, organizations have learned to use many of these methods and tools in their service and administrative areas and therefore refer to this as "Lean Enterprise." Based on the Toyota goals of achieving low cost, high quality and short lead times, Lean focuses on minimizing the time elapsed from receiving the customer's order to providing the product or service.

Many enterprises that have been using Lean are now anxious to take advantage of Six Sigma and, as a result, are looking to integrate the two approaches. The remainder of this chapter will address some of the components of Lean and how they fuse with performance excellence, Six Sigma and business management systems.

The Ford Production System (FPS), which is based on the Toyota Production System and has been promoted as a return to Henry Ford's original vision, is often described as a lean, flexible and disciplined common production system. It stresses applying a set of principles and processes allowing capable and empowered people to learn and work safely together to produce and deliver products that consistently exceed customer expectations in quality, cost and time. Embedded in this approach are many of the common buzzwords and phrases of various past quality movements, plus the new word "lean." This isn't surprising, since lean uses many of the same tools and *programmes du jour* that we have discussed in previous chapters. Let's examine some of them.

1. *What is Total Quality Control? The Japanese Way*, by Professor Kaoru Ishikawa, is a major foundation for what is today referred to as Lean. Ishikawa referred to TQC as a thought revolution in management, saying, "TQC is not a miracle drug, its properties are more like those of a Chinese herb medicine." Some of his other statements were:

    - TQC is management with facts.

    - Set your eyes on long-term profits and put quality first.

    - The next process is your customer.

    - In every work there is dispersion (variation).

    - Data without dispersion is false data.

    - QC begins with a control chart and ends with a control chart.

    - Ninety-five percent of the problems in a company can be solved by the seven tools of QC.

    - Statistical methods must become common knowledge or common sense to all engineers and technicians.

2. *Kaizen: The Key to Japan's Competitive Success* is the title of the work edited by Masaaki Imai in 1986. Mr. Imai says, "Kaizen means gradual, unending improvement, doing 'little things' better, setting and achieving even higher standards." He also says in the acknowledgement, "I must admit that I cannot take credit for all of the ideas expressed in this book. I have merely brought together the management philosophies, theories and tools that have been developed and used over the years in Japan." Kaizen does indeed cover many of the items we have identified as components of Lean. Note that TQC is a major foundation for Kaizen.

Imai also compares Kaizen to innovation. He points to two contrasting approaches, "...the gradualist approach and the great-leap-forward approach. Japanese companies generally favor the gradualist approach and Western companies the great-leap approach..." Even though Six Sigma was not well known when he wrote his book in 1986, his presentation does in fact differentiate innovation/breakthrough/Six Sigma from continual improvement.

One of Imai's arguments is that innovation "is subject to steady deterioration unless continuing efforts are made just to maintain it and then to improve on it." This issue is later addressed in the Six Sigma DMAIC process. Mr. Imai further states, "In reality, there can be no such thing as a static constant. All systems are destined to deteriorate once they have been established. One of the famous Parkinson's Laws is that an organization, once it has built its edifice, begins to decline. In other words, organizations must continually try to improve to even maintain the status quo." Imai further contends that Kaizen is applied closer to production and market while innovation occurs closer to science and technology.

3. *The 5 S's: Five Keys to a Total Quality Environment*, by Takashi Osada, describes the 5 S's, which are intended to eliminate waste:

- **Seiri**: organization/putting things in order.
- **Sieton**: neatness — having things in the right place/layout so they can be used in a hurry.
- **Seiso**: cleaning — getting rid of waste, grime and foreign matter.
- **Seiketsu**: standardization, or continually maintaining organization, neatness and cleanliness.
- **Shitsuke**: discipline — training and the ability to do what you want to do even when it is difficult.

Osada indicates that the 5 S movement, with its emphasis on a clean, well-organized workplace, needs to be the first step before any of the activities of TQC, Kaizen or Quality Circles can begin.

JUST-IN-TIME (JIT)

Toyota's Just-In-Time philosophy is founded on the principle of patience. JIT calls for processes to be confirmed one-by-one, step-by-step. JIT organizations do not proceed to the "next step" until there is a pull (until the next step is requested). The philosophy focuses not only on the quality goal of zero defects, but on a holistic approach that ensures each subprocess' verification, in relation to both its preceding and following subprocesses as well as to the overall business process. The basic concepts of JIT are based on Japan's cultural and economic characteristics.

❖ Japan's lack of natural resources places it at a disadvantage in comparison to Europe and the United States. To overcome this handicap, Toyota felt that it was essential for Japanese industries to produce quality goods with high added values at low production costs — relative to other developed nations.

❖ Japan's emphasis on work as the center of life, its group consciousness and homogenous culture, along with its focus on higher education and self-improvement, provide great economic advantages to industries that allow their workers to exercise their capabilities to the greatest extent possible.

As a result, JIT focuses on achieving low-cost production — on "reducing cost through elimination of waste."

JIT recognizes that any organization that mass produces products (such as automobiles) and assembles thousands of parts that are themselves the products of subprocesses is subject to a common problem: a flaw in any one process will have a major impact on the final product. This realization led to the practice of maintaining large work-in-progress inventories for each process. These were kept to absorb troubles in processes and changes in demand; they were often referred to as "just-in-case inventories." This approach tended to unbalance stock levels between processes and often led to dead stock. Furthermore, it led to a surplus of equipment, space and workers. To counteract the situation, Toyota developed a production system capable of shortening lead time from the arrival of materials to the completion of the vehicle. In the resulting just-in-time method, production lead time is greatly shortened by having "all processes produce the necessary parts at the necessary time" and having on hand only the minimum stock necessary to hold the process together. In addition, by treating inventory quantity and production lead time as policy variables, this production method identifies surplus equipment and workers. This is the starting point of JIT's second characteristic — making full use of worker capabilities. The basic principles of JIT are:

(a) **Withdrawal by subsequent processes** — Every process in a production cycle must be able to quickly gain accurate knowledge of "timing and quantity required."

(b) **One-piece production and conveyance** — Each process must approach the condition of producing only one piece, conveying one piece at a time and retaining only one piece in stock — both between the equipment and processes.

(c) **Leveling of production** — Provided that all processes perform small lot production and conveyance, if the quantity to be withdrawn by the subsequent process varies considerably, the process within the company as well as the suppliers will maintain peak capacity or holding excessive inventory at all times.

(d) **Elimination of waste from overproducing** — The underlying concept is that the value of existing inventory is disavowed.

The following are brief descriptions of some key elements of JIT, which have become part of Lean Enterprise.

JIDOKA

At Toyota, the term means "to make the equipment or operation stop whenever an abnormal or defective condition arises." In short, when equipment trouble or machine defects occur, the equipment or entire line stops — any worker who spots a potential quality problem can stop a line.

KANBAN SYSTEM

The Kanban system uses a form of order card called Kanban, which comes in two kinds — a "conveyance Kanban," which is carried from one subprocess to the *preceding* one, and a "production Kanban," which is used to order production of the portion withdrawn by the *subsequent* subprocess. These two kinds of Kanban are always attached to the containers holding parts. When the contents of a container begin to be used, the conveyance Kanban is removed, and a worker takes it to the stock point of the *preceding* subprocess to pick up the part. The worker then attaches this conveyance Kanban to the container holding the part. Then, the production Kanban is removed and becomes a means of dispatching information for the production process. Each part is produced to replenish the withdrawn part as quickly as possible. Thus, the production activities of the final assembly line are linked to the preceding sub-processes or to the suppliers, and the just-in-time nature of the entire process is maintained.

DOCK TO DOCK (DTD)

DTD is a measure of how fast raw materials are converted to finished goods and shipped. It is not a measure of the speed of the processes, but rather a measure of the time it takes for the material to move through the plant.

ERROR PROOFING

An error is a deviation from a specification. Not all errors are defects, but all defects result from errors. Error proofing is a process improvement that prevents specific defects from occurring.

VISUAL FACILITY

Facilities use visual displays that state the who, what, where, when, why and how of the operation.

QUICK CHANGEOVER

Methods and techniques designed to reduce setup and changeover time, for example the "single-minute exchange of die" (SMED).

VALUE STREAM MAP

A subset of the business process map referred to in Chapter 6. The value stream map focuses on value, differentiating value from waste and getting rid of the waste.

OVERALL EQUIPMENT EFFECTIVENESS (OEE)

OEE measures the availability, the performance efficiency and the quality rate of a given piece of equipment.

The tools listed above represent some of the mechanisms that cumulatively are considered Lean Enterprise. The key component of Lean is Muda – the elimination of waste (non-value-added activities). Some of the weapons are:

❖ Kaizen offensives.

❖ Continual improvement blitzes.

❖ Bottleneck elimination offensives.

These weapons are useful for attacking areas of waste that can be dealt with by applying basic problem-solving tools. Where more sophisticated tools are necessary for breakthrough gains, Six Sigma tools employed by black belts take over.

SIX SIGMA

Many of the concepts of these past and current initiatives are combined in the concept Motorola introduced as "Six Sigma." Six Sigma is like Zero Defects in one particular aspect: it sets stretch goals. "Zero" did not work as a goal, even though Crosby stressed that it was a *direction taken* rather than a *condition achieved*, because it sounded unrealistic. (Crosby countered by saying, "Well, how many defects do you *want* to make? Two? Five?")

In the Six Sigma model, the goal is to reduce the process variation so that the process is *robust* to disturbances. In most cases, a *large* process setback is not a problem because it becomes evident almost immediately. Likewise, *small* process setbacks are not a problem because, even though all variation costs money, small variations generally cost a small amount of money. It is the *inter-*

FIGURE 3-5 WHAT "SIX SIGMA" MEANS

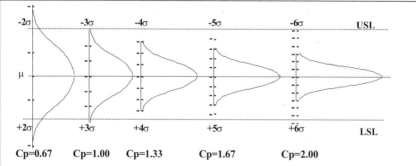

As the process capability improves, defects become less and less likely. Robustness increases as the variation shrinks. Cp is an index of design capability used in some industries.

USL = Upper Specification Limit
LSL = Lower Specification Limit

mediate setbacks that are a problem, since they may go undetected for a time, and during that time, the error rate will increase. Robustness means that even in a worst-case scenario, a process will not produce a substantial number of errors. This can be visualized using the accompanying illustrations (Figures 3-5 and 3-6).

At a three-sigma level of performance, the percentile of the bell curve lying outside the specifications is 0.27 percent, which historically, for most process-es, is effectively zero. However, note that even a small disturbance will shove the bell curve partly outside the acceptable zone. The error rate (defect rate) will increase dramatically for even a small shift. If a process is at the six-sigma level of performance, a shift of 1.5 sigma will result in only a 3.4 parts per mil-lion error rate, or 3.4 defects per million opportunities (DPMO).

Remember, however, that six-sigma quality is just a goal, or a direction. Not even Motorola, which started the program, claims to operate at a six-sigma performance level in every product line and process. As important as the direc-tion is, the methodology for getting there is even more important.

The usual strategy associated with Six Sigma is DMAIC — Define, Measure, Analyze, Improve and Control — an elaboration of Shewhart's PDSA cycle (Figure 3-3). (Motorola did not use the term DMAIC. There is always a danger when thought is reduced to an acronym, since that process is often the first step on the road to rote or mechanical application.) These are

FIGURE 3-6 WHAT SIX SIGMA MEANS

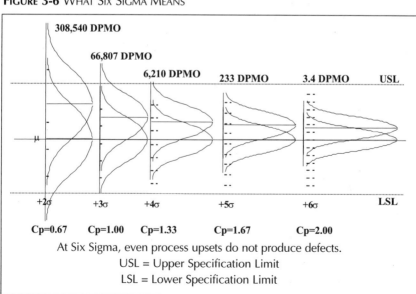

At Six Sigma, even process upsets do not produce defects.
USL = Upper Specification Limit
LSL = Lower Specification Limit

equivalent to five of the eight steps in Ford's 8-D approach and are contained within the three phases of STAT-A-MATRIX's problem-solving approach. The process can really be divided into as many steps as one wishes. When we compare these steps we find that they are very similar. What comprises two "steps" in one approach may comprise a single "step" in another approach.

Define — The nature of the problem (whether existing or potential) must be clearly stated in operational terms. Many people make the mistake of defining the "problem" as the solution or as the suspected cause, saying such things as, "Our problem is communication." It is difficult to see how to solve such a problem.

Measure — Knowledge of the "size and shape" of the problem is required. We not only must know how to measure the problem, but we must know how reliable our measurements are. Finally, we must ask, "Are our measurements directly related to the issue?"

Analyze — The "shape" of the problem is the boundary of what the problem is and is not. The practitioner must ask when the problem happens and when it does not; where and where not; and so on. This is the phase in which most statistical tools come into play. By distinguishing signal from noise in the data, we can identify the clues that point toward probable causes.

Improve — Once a cause is known, an action plan is required. This plan must be crafted to accomplish all of the objectives associated with the original problem — with the time and resources available. This solution must be examined for potential future problems and revised, if necessary. When it is ready, we implement the plan and verify that it works.

Control — Steps are required to "maintain the gain." Otherwise we wind up "solving" the same problems every three years or so. (That is about how long it takes for people to move on, retire, be promoted or just plain forget.) We must focus on irreversible means that depend on human factors as little as possible.

This translates into what Juran called "The Two Journeys." The Diagnostic Journey, from symptom to cause, is the first half of DMAIC; the Remedial Journey, from cause to solution, is the second half.

For planning (or design) problems, some practitioners use the acronym DMADV: Define, Measure, Analyze, Design and Validate. Collectively, DMADV is referred to as Design for Six Sigma (DFSS). Others consider this a needless elaboration. However, planning problems really do require different tools than diagnostic problems. In the DMADV model, *Analyze* can be thought

Figure 3-7 DMAIC vs. DMADV

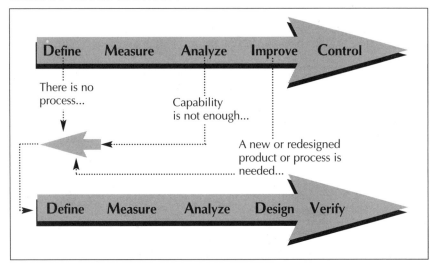

of as constructing a "conceptual design" and *Design* as constructing a "detailed design." *Validate* (some say *verify*) is the testing or "prove-out" of the design. Planning (or design) problems are, in effect, remedial journeys where there is no prior problem to diagnose. With this variety of problem, we identify the potential causes of future problems and incorporate solutions into the plan (design), as shown in Figure 3-7.

Some people say that Six Sigma is TQM on steroids, while others say it is simply a well-deployed TQM process. We define Six Sigma as, "a management philosophy that uses customer-focused measurement and aggressive goal-setting to drive breakthrough performance in demonstrated and validated business results."

First and foremost, Six Sigma is a management philosophy. Unfortunately, many organizations adopting Six Sigma focus exclusively on training so-called black belts and green belts to lead or work on project teams. These organizations fall into the common trap of adopting only a small part of a process. Many programs, as we have seen, have died due to similar partial adoption of a model. In some organizations, black belt certification has become a basic requirement for advancement in management, *regardless of whether or not the skills are actually being applied.* (The recent decisions by the American Society for Quality and the International Quality Federation (IQF) to develop independent and competing black belt certification examinations are, perhaps, evidence that in some instances the title has become more important than the process.)

Second, customer-focused measurement emphasizes listening to the voice of the customer and converting the customer's needs into requirements that can be monitored and measured. This approach helps organizations avoid the pitfall of relying exclusively on internal measures of improvement.

Third, Six Sigma employs a suite of statistical, quantitative and qualitative tools, not just a single set. But Six Sigma adds common measures, such as defects per unit (DPU) and defects per million opportunities (DPMO) and extends these measures to all processes (including transactional and R&D processes) so that every product stage, development or service cycle is subject to measurement on a comparable basis.

Fourth, aggressive goal setting drives breakthrough performance. Unlike prior programs that focused primarily on small, incremental improvements, perhaps of 5 or 10 percent, Six Sigma looks for order of magnitude improvements (10x or more). This does not mean that incremental improvements are not accepted, but it does mean that the focus is on identifying opportunities that yield order of magnitude results.

Fifth, business results are validated. Historically, most programs have used teams to work on improvement projects that reportedly result in savings. However, in the majority of cases, results were never actualized. Six Sigma results must be demonstrated by the financial department as dropping to the bottom line.

SOME SIX SIGMA SUCCESSES

Successful programs are leadership driven. As discussed earlier, the CEO really can't be committed to driving the process unless he or she truly believes in the likelihood of success.

One thing that captures the attention of senior executives is what highly respected CEOs are talking about and publishing in their annual reports, such as business improvement results — validated as dropping to the bottom line as a direct result of Six Sigma projects — amounting to over $2 billion in a single year.

Motorola — Thomas Galvin, chairman of Motorola, initiated Six Sigma as part of the company's strategy to win one of the first Malcolm Baldrige National Quality Awards in 1988. This effort also resulted in Galvin's winning the first Joseph M. Juran Medal from the American Society for Quality in 2000. This medal is awarded to organizational leaders who exhibit a distinguished performance in a sustained role, personally practicing the key principles of quality and demonstrating breakthrough management.

AlliedSignal/Honeywell — Lawrence Bossidy, chairman of the board of AlliedSignal/Honeywell, said in his 1998 annual report, "Six Sigma projects helped boost productivity by 6 percent, spurring an increase in operating margin to a record 13 percent from 11.4 percent last year." In his 1999 annual report, he said, "Growth and productivity go hand in hand at Honeywell. Six Sigma Plus adds elements of the Malcolm Baldrige assessment process to our proven Six Sigma tool kits."

General Electric — Bossidy introduced Six Sigma to his friend Jack Welch, General Electric's past chairman of the board and CEO. GE started Six Sigma in December 1995. Welch said in his 1998 annual report, "We have invested more than $2 billion in effort, and the financial returns have now entered the exponential phase — more than $750 million in savings beyond our investment in 1998." In GE's 1999 annual report, Welch reported, "The Six Sigma initiative is in its fifth year — from a standing start in 1996, it has produced more than $2 billion in benefits in 1999, with much more to come this decade... Six Sigma projects now underway are done on customer processes, many on customer premises." The 2000 GE report had references to Six Sigma accomplishments from each business unit. Some examples are:

GE Power Systems — "Using Six Sigma tools allowed us to ship a record 392 power generation units, a 112 percent increase over 1999 and completed a record 1,434 new unit installations and power plant overhauls. Six Sigma contributed additional capacity at our Greenville, South Carolina, gas turbine plant, where we reduced cycle time by 29 percent, enabling us to increase output by more than 200 percent."

GE Aircraft Engines — "At the heart of everything we do are Six Sigma processes to drive profitability and enhance customer productivity. Six Sigma projects have improved our on-time engine delivery rate to 99 percent. Our 'at the customer, for the customer' program has resulted in more than 1200 customer Six Sigma projects, benefiting airlines worldwide."

GE Medical Systems — "We have completed more than 1,000 Six Sigma projects 'at the customer, for the customer.' These are projects aimed at improving patient throughput and reducing variability in health care delivery. These projects generated more than $100 million in benefits for our customers in 2000 ... GE Medical Systems also introduced 22 Designed for Six Sigma (DFSS) products in 2000. In total, more than 50 percent of our sales will come from DFSS products in 2001."

Other companies introduced to Six Sigma by Jack Welch include American Express and Kodak.

> *American Express* — Kenneth I. Chenoult, president and COO of American Express, reported in his 1999 annual report, "We began to roll out Six Sigma ... in early 1998. Six Sigma projects to date have produced significant process improvement and related savings in a number of areas. Of the 250 projects implemented, 31 were completed by the end of 1999. These 31 projects have produced annualized savings of $10.4 million, or $334,000 per project."

> *Kodak* — George M.C. Fisher, chairman of the board at Kodak, reported in his 1999 annual report, "We have certified more than 300 people in black belt and quality improvement facilitator 2000 programs aimed at moving the organization toward Six Sigma ... more than $100 million can already be attributed to their efforts."

Six Sigma for Small and Medium Enterprises (SMEs) – Many smaller organizations hear about savings in the billions or hundreds of millions of dollars and decide that since their sales are only $10 million or $100 million, Six Sigma doesn't apply to them. They could not be more mistaken. The truth is that small- and medium-sized enterprises, or SMEs, can proportionately gain even greater returns than the large enterprises. Small organizations immediately comment that they are very lean, and with between 10 and 500 employees, their needs can be significantly different. However, these differing needs can be met with modern management tools, as shown by the experiences of Wheelock, Inc.

A SMALLER COMPANY SUCCESS — THE WHEELOCK STORY

For more than 80 years, Wheelock, Inc., of Long Branch, New Jersey, has been a leading supplier of audible and visual signaling devices to the life-safety fire notification market. Wheelock's products are widely recognized for their quality, ease of installation and innovative solutions.

Over the past few decades, Wheelock has become known as a leader in progressive management. Moving from Quality Circles in the 1980s to team-building, education and collaboration initiatives in the 1990s, Wheelock has been recognized on a county, state and national level for its creative approaches to employee relations. The company has spent hundreds of thousands of dollars along with significant investments in energy, time and leadership commitment to shift its culture from individualism to collaboration.

Corporate Philosophy of Improvement — Wheelock has created an environment of learning, teaming and coaching for its employees. It has received multiple New Jersey Department of Labor customized training grants (of more than $700,000) to help fund the Wheelock Enrichment Center, which offers a multifaceted curriculum of corporate education. Wheelock's hard work in this area has paid off handsomely.

❖ Forty classroom hours are budgeted per employee annually.

❖ Productivity increased to more than **118** percent from 105 percent.

❖ Final assembly yields rose to **98** percent from 87 percent.

❖ Turnover is now under **5** percent from well over 30 percent.

❖ On-time delivery improved to **98** percent from 90 percent.

❖ Absenteeism is below **1** percent.

❖ No increase in health insurance premiums for over six years.

Those numbers are impressive, but for Wheelock's CEO and head coach, Peter W. Tarlton, they simply weren't enough. He recognized that if the Wheelock team wanted to be the best in its market niche, it had to improve productivity to the next level, increase profits and delight its internal and external customers to a level never before realized. Wheelock had to learn what the major players were doing to manage differently and more profitably. To accomplish this, top management had to benchmark itself and ask some serious questions.

❖ What companies are doing the right things faster, better and most efficiently?

❖ What is their recipe?

❖ Can a small to midsize manufacturer replicate its results and process?

❖ Can these results be maintained?

❖ Will our culture accept something else new?

Moving Toward Six Sigma ... Plus ISO 9001 — Wheelock's management reviewed the benchmarking data and asked themselves challenging questions: Why not make a concerted effort to pursue Six Sigma with the same energy and dedication as GE, Motorola and AlliedSignal? Why not color outside the box as a small to midsize company? If the results from others are factual, then why shouldn't Wheelock set a target to get the same results? So the company put together an action plan. The budgeted line item initially was for less than $100,000. The business plan called for Doug Phillips, vice president, general operations, and Alan Fazzari, vice president, people services, to deliver a proposal for two initiatives: ISO 9001 and Six Sigma.

In less than 15 months Wheelock:

❖ Trained six associates as black belts.

❖ Trained 15 top and middle managers as champions.

❖ Guided the completion of several process improvement projects with savings close to **$700,000**.

❖ Completed the ISO 9001 training sequence, including lead auditor and internal auditing training.

❖ Completed a Top and Middle Management Empowerment and Facilitation Skills course.

Drawing upon subject-matter experts from my organization, Wheelock also trained its first wave of 15 associates for their green belt certification, trained over 30 associates from multiple functional areas in Design for Six Sigma, held an experiment design class, built a waiting list of associates who wish to be black belts and green belts, completed another wave of facilitation and empowerment training for 20 supervisors, identified more than a dozen black belt projects, worked with the green belts on a dozen other projects and set up a formal Six Sigma/ISO orientation program.

In addition, Wheelock completed several initial projects, with the following savings.

❖ Warehouse Inventory Accuracy $113,000

❖ Kanban Bin Accuracy $31,000

❖ Labeling Inaccuracies $57,000

❖ RG Inefficiencies $4,000

Business plans involving two major Six Sigma projects are also well under way.

Project No. 1: Product Development Cycle Time — The cycle time of product development did not meet customer requirements. The scope of the project was companywide, and Wheelock was going to analyze three recent product-development cycles (PDCs). The PDC project initially began in the following manner.

❖ A team of middle managers was formed.

❖ Executive level meetings took place to discuss product development.

❖ Themes were created from these meetings.

❖ An action plan was developed to address challenges associated with these themes.

Immediately, an "As-Is" process map was put together and agreed to by the executive team. Approximately 35 "issues" came forth, ranging from incomplete preparation for agency approval to manufacturability of the product under development. The strongest theme, however, was that *the PDC process was not truly a collaborative effort*; "silos" had been built.

The "As-Is" process flow showed more than 75 activities with a minimum time of 239 days and a maximum time of 1,779 days. Prior to February 2001 (the start of the project), functions other than engineering were not adequately involved until more than 50 percent of the cycle of activities had been completed — sometimes 800 work days.

Trend analysis showed Wheelock hit completion dates (milestones) less than 80 percent of the time. Certain specifications were either not completed or poorly developed, which caused confusion as one group handed their work product to the next group.

One area that immediately caught the attention of the project leader was the plethora of Engineering Change Notices (ECNs), representing a large pool of "non-value-added" activities. The average processing cost was $577 per ECN without a design component; with a design component, the cost was $3,214 per ECN. In four-and-a-half years, Wheelock documented 2,293 ECNs at a cost of processing close to $303,000 a year.

Other areas of concern included an overreliance on design aspects learned during pilot runs. The voice of Wheelock's internal customers (VOC) wasn't at Six Sigma levels. Codependencies didn't exist, costing as much as $500,000 in additional costs because of "relooping" prior to major product launches. Product design reviews and "matter of viewpoint" product safety meetings were held after pilot runs, but such reviews needed to be held earlier, more frequently and conducted in greater detail.

Wheelock achieved the following goals.

❖ Core product multidisciplinary teams now meet at last two times per week.

❖ A Customer Delight Council has been created, whose primary focus is VOC (voice of the external customer).

❖ The "Should-Be" process map now has only 17 activities, which include two all-inclusive pilot runs and multiple viewpoint checks and balances.

❖ There are two primary objectives being pursued: robust designs using Six Sigma tools and decreased time to market (to meet customer requirements).

❖ Multidisciplinary teams remain involved with a project from its marketing specification stage to the product launch date.

Project No. 2: Reducing Touch-up Time (time spent on touch-up soldering for its printed circuit boards) — Just about everything Wheelock makes requires a printed circuit board. Demand for its latest family of fire notification strobes was starting to take off. A slow production problem was attributed to one operation: touch-up soldering costs were too high for its printed circuit boards. Just how high were they? They accounted for 27 percent of the total assembly labor and more than $144,000 annually — just on one series of boards! The test yields before touch-up operations were just below 90 percent.

Wheelock's goal was to determine the root cause of defective boards and to recommend corrective actions that would reduce or eliminate the need for soldering. What did the company find? It confirmed that certain component leads were too long, contributing to solder bridges and/or voids between leads. Some components were not fully seated and the level of ownership of the overall process was not optimum.

To rectify this, the company mapped the entire process and began to evaluate and eliminate non-value-added steps — lead trimming and staging work for test. Wheelock also applied SPC to its wave-solder process, ran designed experiments (DOE) on its wave solder parameters and contacted flux and solder suppliers.

The company also formed work cells and new teams, in which the team owned the entire process. Each team was responsible for hand insertion, wave solder, touch-up and test. Wheelock was delighted by the resulting enthusiasm; as management increased its level of interest, the workers followed suit.

With the application of SPC (by a wave-solder operator) and DOE, the process achieved high levels of control and was applied to all printed circuit boards. Wheelock found that there were better yields without touch-up (95 percent) and that led to extraordinary results: the elimination of eight touch-up operations and two rework operations and the elimination of the "doop loop" (the constant circle that a product goes into due to rework of one kind or another during production). These changes resulted in annual savings of $435,000. The intangible results included team ownership, along with a sense of pride and a competitive spirit. Especially satisfying for Wheelock: Two machine operators signed on for more extensive training, leading to green belt certification.

CHAMPIONING IMPROVEMENT

Wheelock's successes demonstrate that the benefits of modern quality initiatives, such as Six Sigma, can be valuable even to smaller companies. Wheelock's executive team understands that to continually improve upon its 80-year reputation for quality, it must be aware of and positively influence the factors that really matter in business — the voices of external and internal customers. And, by building Six Sigma into an ISO 9001 base, Wheelock is structuring a management system that will maintain gains. In short, by considering ISO 9001 and Six Sigma as complementary aspects of a total business system, Wheelock has moved toward Fusion Management, as we will describe in later chapters.

4

Fusing Performance Excellence, Six Sigma and Quality Management Systems

An organization may have a structure and a dynamic — or effective management system and a suitable continual improvement process — and still be lacking. The third element of Fusion Management is the use of excellence criteria to establish *direction* for an organization. Six Sigma partially fills this role by providing tactical goals for specific organizational processes, but it does not go far enough. In contrast, performance excellence models can provide the multifaceted guidelines that every organization needs to be successful. We chose to *fuse* the Malcolm Baldrige National Award criteria to our system because it does the best job of identifying the values and concepts that lead to organizational excellence. In this chapter, we will discuss the Baldrige criteria at great length because they provide the strategic component and ultimate measure of what Fusion Management is all about.

THE MALCOLM BALDRIGE NATIONAL QUALITY AWARD

The Malcolm Baldrige National Quality Award (MBNQA) was created in the United States by Public Law 100-107 signed on August 20, 1987. The award program led to the creation of a new partnership between government and industry. The award is presented by the Department of Commerce through the National Institute of Standards and Technology (NIST) and managed by the American Society for Quality. Principal support for the program comes from the Foundation for the Malcolm Baldrige National Quality Award established in 1988.

When the Baldrige process was introduced, the program literature clearly stated that the criteria were nonprescriptive. Recognizing that there are many different ways in which an enterprise can succeed, the award committee specified performance criteria, not methodology. In this chapter, using these criteria as a baseline, we will evaluate models for performance excellence and consider how they relate to other aspects of quality management.

The core values and concepts for the 2002 Baldrige award are embodied in seven categories.

    1. Leadership.

    2. Strategic Planning.

    3. Customer and Market Focus.

    4. Information and Analysis.

    5. Human Resource Focus.

    6. Process Management.

    7. Business Results.

These categories are shown in a systems perspective in Figure 4-1. Figure 4-2 shows how Six Sigma relates to the seven Baldrige criteria.

FIGURE 4-1 BALDRIGE CRITERIA FRAMEWORK: A SYSTEMS PERSPECTIVE

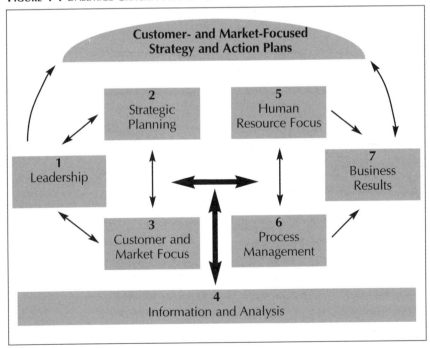

FIGURE 4-2 SIX SIGMA AND THE SEVEN BALDRIGE CRITERIA

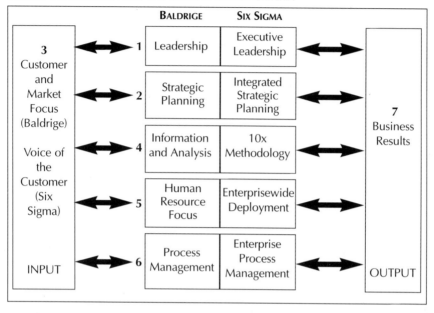

These criteria have changed (or evolved) over the years. The categories were renumbered, *not* in order of importance, but in an order that seemed to make logical sense, as illustrated in the schematics in Figures 4-1 and 4-2. A comparison of the 1988 to the 2002 criteria is shown in Figure 4-3.

FIGURE 4-3 COMPARISON OF AWARD CATEGORIES AND POINT VALUES (2002, 1988)

2002 Number and Title	Points	1988 Number and Title	Points
1. Leadership	120	1. Leadership	150
2. Strategic Planning	85	3. Strategic Quality Planning	75
3. Customer and Market Focus	85	7. Customer Satisfaction	300
4. Information and Analysis	90	2. Information and Analysis	75
5. Human Resource Focus	85	4. Human Resource Utilization	150
6. Process Management	85	5. QA of Products and Services	150
7. Business Results	450	6. Results from Quality Analysis	100
Total Points	**1,000**	**Total Points**	**1,000**

The most striking change is that the words "quality" and "quality assurance/QA" have been deleted from the 2002 version. Thus, *Strategic Quality Planning* of 1988 becomes *Strategic Planning* in 2002, while *QA of Products and Services* becomes *Process Management*. *Results from Quality Analysis* becomes *Business Results*. This is an attempt to show how quality is integrated into the overall drive for excellence in performance. As noted earlier, there is no such thing as quality without cost. If an enterprise's leadership doesn't recognize that results are achieved by faithfully generating the product features (qualities) that satisfy or delight customers at a reasonable price, the enterprise is probably not a serious contender to win the award.

Earlier measures required results to be directly attributable to quality assurance efforts. This encouraged organizations to focus on classical measures of quality, such as percent defective, scrap, rework, etc. These are internal measures that may or may not relate to organizational excellence. We may, for example, successfully eliminate all scrap on a product that doesn't sell. (This would mean we have worked on the wrong project.) Current measures focus on return on investment (ROI) and profit and loss (P&L). On the surface, this change may cause people to question the relationship of performance excellence to continual improvement. Six Sigma, the current improvement model, emphasizes defects per million opportunities (DPMO) and cycle time reduction, both internal measures. However, Six Sigma also places heavy emphasis on choosing projects that are related to business issues. Whatever internal measures are used to analyze and track these projects, the end result must "drop to the bottom line," as validated by the financial department. Since publicly traded Baldrige Award recipients have outperformed the Standard and Poor's 500 by four to one, there must be *some* connection between performance excellence and business results.

Annual analyses of the effectiveness of various subcategories in the assessment have resulted in a reduction from 42 to 18 subcategories within the seven core categories. The changes have been significant.

BUSINESS RESULTS (CATEGORY 7)

Perhaps the most significant change to any one category from the 1988 to the 2002 criteria involves recasting *Results from Quality Analysis*, which had a maximum value of 100 points, to *Business Results* with a whopping 450 points. This change is partly due to the influence of the European Quality Award, but also to the financial difficulties encountered by several former Baldrige winners shortly after winning. While the ensuing publicity led a number of people to question the value of the award, the primary rationale for the shift stemmed from a growing awareness that it was time to speak the language of management and focus on key business indicators. The subcategories for Business Results (year 2002) include:

7.1 Customer-focused results	125 points
7.2 Financial and market results	125 points

7.3 Human resource results   80 points

7.4 Organizational effectiveness results   120 points

Please note: The category descriptions in this chapter are taken from the 2002 Baldrige Criteria for Performance Excellence.

The Business Results category provides a results focus that encompasses a customer evaluation of products and services, a review of overall financial and market performance and the results of all key process improvement activities. This focus emphasizes a superior value of offerings as viewed by your customers and the marketplace, superior organizational performance as reflected in operational and financial indicators and organizational and personal learning. Category 7 thus provides "real-time" information (measures of progress) for evaluation and improvement of processes, products and services, in alignment with overall organizational strategy. Item 7.1 calls for analysis of business results data and information to determine overall organizational performance.

7.1 Customer-Focused Results

Purpose — This item addresses an organization's customer-focused performance results, with the aim of demonstrating how well the organization has been satisfying customers and delivering product and service quality that lead to satisfaction, loyalty and positive referral.

7.2 Financial and Market Results

Purpose — This item focuses on an organization's financial and market results, with the aim of understanding marketplace challenges and opportunities.

7.3 Human Resource Results

Purpose — This item targets human resource results, with the aim of demonstrating how well an organization has been creating and maintaining a positive, productive, learning and caring work environment for all employees.

7.4 Organizational Effectiveness Results

Purpose — This section examines an organization's other key operational performance results with regard to achieving organizational effectiveness, attaining key organizational goals and demonstrating good organizational citizenship.

CUSTOMER AND MARKET FOCUS (CATEGORY 3)

Customer Satisfaction, which was worth 300 points in 1988, has now become *Customer and Market Focus,* for only 85 points. Although change appears to deemphasize customer satisfaction, note that 125 of the 450 points for Business Results are based on customer-focused results while another 125 points of the 450 are for financial and market results — all indications of customer satisfaction. Overall, the point values are not only consistent with regard to customer satisfaction, but the 2002 criteria more clearly define how those points should be earned. Subcategories for Customer and Market Focus are:

3.1 Customer and market knowledge   40 points

3.2 Customer relationships and satisfaction   45 points

Customer and Market Focus addresses how well an organization seeks to understand the voices of customers and of the marketplace. This category stresses the importance of relationships in overall listening, learning and performance excellence strategy. Customer satisfaction and dissatisfaction results provide vital information for understanding customers and the marketplace. In many cases, such results and trends provide the most meaningful information, not only on customer views but also on marketplace behavior — that is, repeat business and positive referrals.

3.1 Customer and Market Knowledge

Purpose — This section addresses an organization's key process for gaining knowledge about current and future customers and their markets, with the aim of offering relevant products and services, understanding emerging customer requirements/expectations and keeping pace with marketplace changes, including changing ways of doing business.

3.2 Customer Relationships and Satisfaction

Purpose — This area focuses on an organization's processes for building customer relationships and determining customer satisfaction, with the aim of acquiring new customers, retaining existing customers and developing new market opportunities.

Customer and market knowledge cause us not only to consider today's customers, but to look forward to tomorrow's customers. Many companies focus only on existing (or former) customers that complain, while being woefully ignorant of the silent majority. Meanwhile, there are dissatisfied customers who do not complain and customers that are satisfied who we seldom hear from. *Why are they satisfied?* There are customers of our competitors. *Why aren't they our customers?* And there are those customers who aren't ours or our competitors — but could be. It has been said that the most significant customers are the ones we don't yet have. To depend only on customer complaints for "market knowledge" is like camping in the jungle for a night and making risk assumptions based solely on the animals that creep within the light of your campfire on that particular night. Odds are that you're going to overlook a few important species that may one day cost you a limb — or worse.

STRATEGIC PLANNING (CATEGORY 2)

Strategic Quality Planning (75 points) in 1988 was changed to *Strategic Planning* (85 points) in 2002. Although the title and maximum point value assigned to this category changed little, the focus has shifted to overall strategic planning. We call this *integrated strategic planning*, a unique approach to focusing managerial breakthrough that *fuses* strategic business plans with strategic quality and strategic regulatory plans. By fusing all three plans, an organization can focus on two subcategories:

2.1 Strategy development   40 points

2.2 Strategy deployment   45 points

Strategic Planning addresses strategic and action planning, as well as the deployment of plans. This category stresses that customer-driven quality and operational performance are key strategic issues that need to be integral to an organization's overall planning.

2.1 Strategy Development

Purpose — This item examines how an organization sets strategic directions and develops strategic objectives, guiding and strengthening overall performance and competitiveness.

2.2 Strategy Deployment

Purpose — This item examines how an organization converts strategic objectives into action plans and how it assesses progress relative to them. The aim is to ensure that strategies are deployed for goal achievement.

> *Note: As discussed in many places in this book, lack of deployment is a key reason for failure of many programmes du jour.*

HUMAN RESOURCE FOCUS (CATEGORY 5)

Human Resource Utilization (150 points) in 1988 became *Human Resource Focus* (85 points) in 2002. On the surface, this appears to be a 65-point decrease, but when we factor in subcategory 7.3, Human Resource Results (80 points), we see that, in effect, the emphasis on people has really increased by 15 points from 1988. The subcategories for this category are:

5.1 Work systems	35 points
5.2 Employee education, training and development	25 points
5.3 Employee well-being and satisfaction	25 points

Human Resource Focus addresses key human resource practices — those directed toward creating and maintaining a high-performance workplace and an educable employee base that enables an organization to adapt to change. This category covers human resource development and management requirements in an integrated way, i.e., aligned with an organization's strategic objectives. Human resource focus includes work environment and employee support climate.

To reinforce the basic alignment of human resource management with overall strategy, the criteria include human resource planning in the overall planning section of the Strategic Planning category.

5.1 Work Systems

Purpose — This item looks at an organization's systems for work and jobs, compensation, employee performance management, motivation, recognition, communication and hiring, with the aim of enabling and encouraging all employees to contribute effectively and to the best of their ability. These systems are intended to foster high performance, to result in individual and organizational learning and to enable adaptation to change.

5.2 Employee Education, Training and Development

Purpose — This section focuses on the education, training and on-the-job reinforcement of work force knowledge and skills within the context of meeting ongoing employee needs and creating a high-performance workplace.

5.3 Employee Well-Being and Satisfaction

Purpose — This section examines an organization's work environment, employee support climate and how employee satisfaction is determined with the aim of fostering well-being, satisfaction and motivation of all employees while recognizing their diverse needs.

PROCESS MANAGEMENT (CATEGORY 6)

Quality Assurance of Products and Services (150 points) in 1988 was changed to *Process Management* (85 points) in 2002. The United States has undergone a transformation from needing to improve the quality of its products and services to recognizing that competitiveness and performance excellence require a focus on managing the business process. This is evidenced not only in performance excellence but also in quality management systems like ISO 9001:2000 and Six Sigma. The subcategories for Process Management are:

6.1 Product and service processes	45 points
6.2 Business processes	25 points
6.3 Support processes	15 points

Process Management is the focal point of all the criteria for key work processes. Built into this category are the central requirements for efficient and effective process management: effective design, prevention orientation, linkage to suppliers and partners, supply chain integration, improved operational performance, reduced cycle time, ongoing evaluation, continual improvement and organizational learning.

Agility, cost reduction and cycle time reduction are becoming increasingly important in all aspects of process management and organizational design. In simple terms, "agility" refers to the ability to adapt quickly, flexibly and effectively to changing requirements. Depending on the nature of an organization's strategy and markets, agility might imply rapid change from one product to another, rapid response to changing demands or the ability to produce a wide range of customized services. Agility may also involve outsourcing decisions, agreements with key suppliers and novel partnering arrangements. Flexibility might demand special strategies, such as modular designs, shared components and manufacturing lines and specialized training. Cost and cycle time reduction often involves agile process management strategies. It is crucial to have key measures for tracking all aspects of overall process management.

6.1 Product and Service Processes

Purpose — This section examines key product and service design and delivery processes, with the aim of improving marketplace and operational performance.

6.2 Business Processes

Purpose — This requirement examines key nonproduct/nonservice business processes, with the aim of improving business success.

6.3 Support Processes

Purpose — This item examines key support processes, with the aim of improving overall operational performance.

LEADERSHIP (CATEGORY 1)

For the two remaining criteria, the titles have not changed and the point changes are negligible.

Leadership, from 150 to 120 points — The subcategories are:

1.1 Organizational leadership	80 points
1.2 Public responsibility and citizenship	40 points

Leadership addresses how senior leaders guide the organization in setting organizational values, direction and performance expectations. Attention is given to how senior leaders communicate with employees, how they review organizational performance and create an environment that encourages high performance. This category also includes responsibilities to the public and how an organization practices good citizenship.

1.1 Organizational Leadership

Purpose — This item examines the key aspects of an organization's leadership and the actions of senior leaders to create and sustain a high-performance organization.

1.2 Public Responsibility and Leadership

Purpose — This section examines how an organization fulfills its public responsibilities and encourages, supports and practices good citizenship.

INFORMATION AND ANALYSIS (CATEGORY 4)

Information and Analysis, from 75 to 90 points — The subcategories are:

4.1 Measurement and analysis of organizational performance	50 points
4.2 Information management	40 points

The Information and Analysis category is the main point within the criteria for all key information about effectively measuring and analyzing performance to drive improvement and organizational competitiveness. In simple terms, Category 4 is the "brain center" for the alignment of an organization's operations and strategic objectives. Central to such use of data and information is quality and availability. Since information and analysis can be primary sources of competitive advantage and productivity growth, this category includes such strategic considerations.

4.1 Measurement and Analysis of Organizational Performance

Purpose — This subcategory focuses on the selection, management and use of data and information for performance measurement and analysis in support of organizational planning and performance improvement. It is a central collection and analysis point in an integrated performance measurement and management system that relies on financial and nonfinancial data and information. The aim of measurement and analysis is to guide an organization's process management toward the achievement of key business results and strategic objectives.

4.2 Information Management

Purpose — This item examines how an organization ensures the availability of high-quality, timely data and information for all key users — employees, suppliers/partners and customers.

NATIONAL, STATE AND LOCAL AWARDS

There are at least 44 states in the United States that have quality awards fashioned after Baldrige as of this writing. Nearly 60 countries also have some form of national quality award, several of which are direct descendents of the Baldrige criteria, while others have been adapted from Baldrige or have evolved in parallel with Baldrige. Figure 4-4 shows some statistics of 54 award programs in the United States representing national, state and local award initiatives, receiving a combined total of more than 600 applications in a single year.

Consider the number of corporations that have internal awards based on Baldrige and the number of US government agencies pursuing the President's

FIGURE **4-4** 2001 STATE, REGIONAL AND LOCAL QUALITY AWARD STATISTICS

Programs	Examiners Trained	Applications Received	Criteria Distributed	Total No. of States Covered
54	2,456[1]	609[2]	48,449[3]	44

Total Number of Programs Reporting = 41
  [1]Four programs of those reporting data did not report on this item.
  [2]Five programs of those reporting data did not report on this item.
  [3]Ten programs of those reporting data did not report on this item. This total
    does not include the number of criteria distributed through the Internet (i.e.,
    number of hits, downloads from program web sites).
Source: NIST Baldrige National Quality Program

Award, which is based on similar criteria. Add to that the awards in health care and education and we can see that such performance-based excellence models are becoming an important tool for evaluating organizational success.

In the remainder of this chapter, we discuss the relationship of quality management systems, continual improvement and performance excellence models.

THE HIERARCHY OF EXCELLENCE APPROACHES

If we look at performance excellence, Six Sigma, Lean, TQM (continual improvement) and management systems, we see that each represents a different level in a hierarchical structure of the business process (Figure 4-5). This structure is best understood in terms of what we are measuring and where we are measuring it.

FIGURE 4-5 HIERARCHY FOR FUSION MANAGEMENT

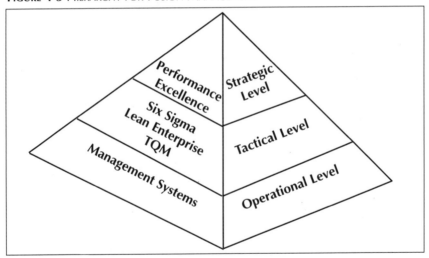

Performance excellence models are able to function equally well for manufacturing, service, health care, education, government and small enterprises because the assessment criteria focus on a short list of critical elements. Baldrige has seven elements, while the European counterpart — European Quality Award (EQA), managed by the European Foundation for Quality Management (EFQM) — has nine elements (four of which are "results"). Although the number of elements differs, the factors measured are essentially the same.

Prior to the establishment of the MBNQA and the EQA, greater emphasis was placed on error rates, returns, percent defective, process aim (process control) and process variability (capability) — in other words, on the everyday performance of existing operations. In most cases, these measures were not easily aligned with business success: profit, time to market, return on investment, customer satisfaction, etc.

The inability to correlate quality performance measures and business performance objectives led to communication breakdowns in many enterprises. Senior executives and operational personnel were working towards nonaligned goals and essentially speaking different languages. Six Sigma applies measures such as defects per million opportunities (DPMO) to all processes and ensures correlation of these measures with business results by requiring that each project demonstrate actual results measured and validated as reaching the bottom line. Moreover, the use of DPMO as a common measure, applicable to all processes and services, makes Six Sigma an excellent tool to support performance excellence goals.

But even these measures offer only a partial view of the whole. Successful organizations do more than excel at what they have always done. When our focus is too immediate and too local, we lose sight of the larger picture. For example, the accounting department of one large company "improved" its processing time by "farming out" much of its work to other operations within the company. The same amount of time (or more) was being spent on accounting, but it was no longer being measured and recorded. Hence, it became difficult to evaluate and improve the company's accounting operations. In another example, a purchasing department "cut costs" by purchasing a less expensive version of an ingredient requested by a process engineer. The cheaper item broke down in the final process, resulting in rejection of the finished product, delivery delays

FIGURE 4-6 COMPARISON OF MBNQA, SIX SIGMA AND ISO 9001:2000

MBNQA Category	Six Sigma	ISO 9001:2000
1. Leadership	Management Champions	Management Reponsibility
2. Strategic Planning	Project Planning	Quality Planning
3. Customer and Market Focus	Voice of the Customer	Customer Focus
4. Information and Analysis	DMAIC/DMADV	Measurement, Analysis and Improvement
5. Human Resource Focus	Black Belt and Green Belt Training	Resource Management
6. Process Management	Project Management	Product Realization
7. Business Results	Project Results	Quality Results

and substantially higher overall costs. Excellence criteria focus on broad, enterprisewide measures and complete the Fusion Management hierarchy.

Figure 4-6 shows the key relationships among performance excellence, continual improvement and management system elements by comparing similarities of MBNQA, Six Sigma and ISO 9001:2000.

Note that performance excellence (via MBNQA) focuses on business results, while Six Sigma emphasizes project results as a critical element. ISO 9001:2000, on the other hand, does not directly address bottom-line results, but addresses continual improvement and process approval. Although the emphasis on management responsibility has been strengthened by taking into account "management commitment" and "customer focus," the standard remains focused on management *accountability* and *involvement* rather than on actual *leadership*. These differences in emphasis create the need for Fusion Management.

BALDRIGE CRITERIA AND HOW THEY RELATE TO THE HIERARCHY

In the following subsections, we will examine each of the seven 2002 Baldrige criteria and how each of the three approaches relates to that criterion.

1. LEADERSHIP

While performance excellence and Six Sigma both focus on leadership, ISO 9001:2000 stresses management responsibility and commitment to quality. The difference is significant. Strong leadership involves clearly defined vision and missions. It requires that executives demonstrate personal involvement by dedicating their own time and providing the necessary resources to ensure the achievement of their missions. The ISO 9001 requirement to define and demonstrate management responsibility and commitment represents a much lower level of involvement. Consider the following example.

Several years ago I was in the office of the CEO of a large French enterprise, discussing the *process for excellence* that we were about to initiate. Our task over the next few weeks was to visit each of the seven business unit heads to obtain their input and ensure that they were committed to the process we were going to create together. As we were about to close the meeting with the CEO, he asked if I needed anything. I responded that I needed him to be prepared for a significant commitment.

"But of course," he said. "Have I not provided for the budget and the availability of each of our business unit's senior staff to meet with you as you requested?"

My response was that I needed something more precious than money; I needed his time. "But of course. Did I not spend this evening with you, preparing you for your meetings?"

I explained that I appreciated his efforts to date, but that, for this enterprise to succeed, he had to be prepared to commit 40 hours per month, focusing on his organization's managerial breakthrough process.

With that, this 6′ 3″ executive turned pale, jumped to his feet, slammed his fist on the conference table and exclaimed, *"Mon Dieu!"* After he calmed down we spent two more hours discussing the significance of this request and the fact that the most common failure in management efforts such as this stems from a lack of executive leadership. By the end of our conversation he came around. "You will explain to each president that he will need to devote 40 hours per month providing leadership on this effort," he agreed.

"And you?" I pressed.

"Yes, I will commit 40 hours per month also."

I never really knew how many hours were spent by these top executives, but it was enough to be successful (at least until the company was acquired by another very large enterprise).

2. STRATEGIC PLANNING

The next criterion is strategic planning. Our approach is to combine the strategic business, quality and regulatory plans of a company into a single *integrated strategic plan*. Typically, business improvement initiatives fail because one or more of the constituent parts of a strategic business plan are unsuccessful. We have all heard individuals working on team improvement projects say, "I can't work on this project any longer, I have *real work* to do." The implication is that the project is not a priority — not associated with the strategic business plan — and therefore can be dropped, or at least set aside.

The objective of an integrated strategic plan (business, quality and regulatory) is to ensure that every significant activity or project is evaluated in terms of its contribution to the achievement of the organization's strategic objectives. Performance excellence models and Six Sigma improvement goals define the need for strategic planning; our goal is to integrate strategic business, quality and regulatory plans. (Note that ISO 9001:2000 does not address strategic plan-

Figure 4-7 Integration of Strategic Business, Quality and Regulatory Plans

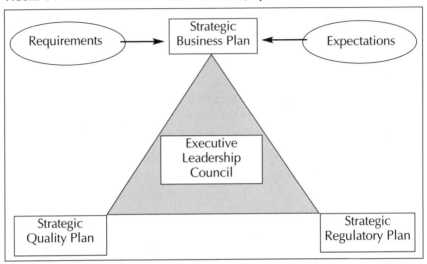

ning at all — only quality planning and product realization planning.) Figure 4-7 illustrates the integration of business, quality and regulatory plans. The importance of strategic planning will be discussed more fully later in this chapter.

3. Customer and Market Focus

Have you ever heard individuals in your organization or in a bank or retail shop say that if it weren't for the customers, their job would be easy? Today, it is obvious to most people that if we don't satisfy our customers they will go someplace else. For many decades, this truism was either overlooked or taken for granted. Today, however, we frequently hear people talking about "exceeding customer expectations" and "delighting the customer."

Fusion Management employs aspects of performance excellence and Six Sigma to exceed customer expectations. Both systems emphasize the use of such tools as voice of the customer (VOC) and quality function deployment (QFD) for achieving customer satisfaction. These tools are generally taught as part of black belt training and provide a means of interpreting customer expectations and design for Six Sigma customer satisfaction. Explicit new language with regard to customer focus, as we have noted, was incorporated into ISO 9001:2000, but it is difficult for organizations to address this topic at the management system (operational) level.

There are many stories about organizations like Nordstrom, the upscale department store that empowers its employees to do whatever it takes to satisfy the customer. I recall one story in which a department store employee arranged to handle the return of defective tires for a customer. This was unusual since the store did not sell tires. Another story tells of an employee in the store's dress department waiting on a customer who had just recovered from surgery. Her husband told her to buy a special dress since they were going out. When the customer took out her charge card, the employee told her to put it away; the dress would be a gift from the store.

These stories certainly illustrate the notion of delighting the customer, but are they good business? How does one create an even balance between customer satisfaction and business results?

Let's revisit the case of the woman recovering from surgery.

- ❖ Could the salesperson still have delighted the customer by charging her for the dress and offering to buy a complementary accessory?
- ❖ Does the store have any limit on how much of a gift a salesperson may give without approval of a higher authority?

While you contemplate these two questions, let me explain that I learned about these unusual incidents in my local newspaper when a new Nordstrom department store was being built in the area. The store couldn't have purchased a more effective ad, even if it had spent 5 to 10 times the cost of the dress. Having said that, if every salesperson followed the same approach, would there be a balance between customer satisfaction and business results? *This balance is one that each organization must determine for itself.*

As a side note, last year, a week before Christmas, my wife reported that the service at our local Nordstrom was still superb and that the store was a wonderful place to shop, but that the crowds there were small in comparison to the other stores in the mall. Moreover, a news program reported that the local Nordstrom was modifying its merchandising approaches to help capture a segment of the marketplace that its stores had failed to secure in the past. This is another example of failing to understand customer needs. It brings us back to our discussion of Shewhart's focus on understanding customer wants and designing products to satisfy those wants. Today, we use tools such as voice of the customer and quality function deployment as vehicles to help us achieve such understanding.

4. INFORMATION AND ANALYSIS

Information and analysis is the next criterion addressed by performance excellence. ISO 9001:2000 addresses information, analysis and improvement. There is, however, a significant difference between *data* and *information*, although many people think of them as synonymous. *Data* is comprised of recorded observations. *Information* is the product of subjecting a number of data points to examination, analysis and interpretation. Information helps us to make effective decisions and take appropriate actions. Six Sigma utilizes various tool application models to generate not 5 and 10 percent improvements, but 10x (order of magnitude) business result improvements. This 10x improvement is one of the criteria that differentiates Six Sigma from previous approaches to improvement. In Fusion Management we always refer to information-driven decision making.

5. Human Resources

Fusion Management demands that an organization use all of its resources, including its human resources, as effectively and efficiently as possible. As discussed previously, performance excellence focuses on human resources. ISO 9001:2000 addresses resource management, while Six Sigma addresses human resources by focusing on assigning full-time trained black belts to work on Six Sigma projects as project team leaders. Six Sigma also uses team members who may work part-time on projects and who have been trained as green belts. Furthermore, the executive team is trained to serve as mentors and champions who, in conjunction with trained master black belts, ensure the smooth deployment of the Six Sigma process.

6. Process Management

Originally, MBNQA focused on "Quality Assurance of Products and Services." To relate this part of ISO 9001:2000 to the Baldrige Criteria, ISO 9001:2000 is roughly analagous to the Process Management category in the MBNQA — in short, if you have a documented, audited, verifiable quality management system with an effective continual improvement process, you are meeting that aspect of a performance excellence model. Another way of looking at it is shown in Figure 4-5: process management is part of the management system level of the Fusion Management hierarchy.

7. Business Results

Business results are the final criterion, but they are of the greatest significance to a business's success and the Fusion Management process. Initially, the MBNQA focused on quality results (1988), then quality and operational results (1992) and more recently, business results (1995). You can see from Figure 4-8 that the number of points (on a scale of 1,000 points) originally designated for quality results has climbed from 150 in 1988 to 450 in 2002.

Figure 4-8 Weighting of Results in MBNQA Criteria

Time Period	Points	Category
1988-1990	150	Quality Results
1991-1991	180	Quality Results
1992-1994	180	Quality and Operational Results
1995-1996	250	Business Results
1997-2002	450	Business Results

This change in emphasis represents an evolution in the thinking process. It demonstrates that "good intentions" are laudable, but that business results are the real measures of success. These business results should be validated by the enterprise's financial/accounting operation; they should yield a measurably favorable net result (a "profit" in a for-profit business environment). Figure 4-6 outlined the similarities and differences between performance excellence, Six Sigma (managerial breakthrough) and management systems. *The successful integration of these three process approaches is Fusion Management.*

Strategic Planning — Key to Performance Excellence

Most companies spend a significant amount of time, energy and money on their strategic business plans, yet in many cases, only a few people ever get to see them. This tends to be out of fear that:

- ❖ Competitors may get their hands on sensitive business information.
- ❖ Employees may not understand the context in which the plan was developed.

Unfortunately, for small to midsize companies and the individual facilities of larger enterprises, management teams often don't participate in the development of the plan nor do they ever see the plan. This makes the plan difficult to follow. Factors that may be considered in the planning process are discussed below.

Part of any strategic plan is an internal analysis of the organization's Strengths, Weaknesses, Opportunities and Threats — SWOT. The leadership council of the enterprise brainstorms each of these four questions.

1. What are the *strengths* of the enterprise that truly differentiate it from its competition? What about the enterprise is unique — in terms of technology, methodology, people resources, process resources, leadership, quality and services?

2. What are the enterprise's *weaknesses*? A lack of new products? Inadequate product development? An inadequate supply chain? Outdated technology? Poor customer service/quality/cycle time?

3. What are the enterprise's *opportunities*? New or improved products or services? New technology? New markets?

4. What are the *threats* to the enterprise that place it behind competitors or could lead to loss of business or reduction in gross profit? Current strong products that could become commodities, or could be phased out? Lack of new products in the pipeline? Customer plans to build rather than buy? Key suppliers going out of business? Economy causing reduced demand?

Benchmarking — Key Element in Strategic Planning — Benchmarking is essential to the success of the Fusion Management system. For many years, when people discussed benchmarking, they spoke about comparing themselves to their competition, and about how difficult, if not impossible, it was to do. In the mid-1980s, with the start of the Baldrige Award, people began to understand the concept of benchmarking against best in class. Such a process requires that an organization consider each subprocess that it wishes to improve, identify who is the best at this subprocess and benchmark against that enterprise or group of enterprises. For example, if we were considering the distribution process, irrespective of what and how we currently distribute, we would consider companies such as Federal Express and L.L. Bean for benchmarking.

Strategic Quality Plan — Fusion Management also requires that we address the integration of strategic planning, that is, the integration of the strategic business, quality and regulatory plans, as shown in Figure 4-7. Most organizations address the quality plan by adding a sentence or two in the strategic business plan that says the company is committed to high quality and customer satisfaction. However, in most of these cases, nobody addresses the plan(s) for:

❖ Identifying the customer.

❖ Determining customer needs and wants.

❖ Converting customer needs and wants into measurable characteristics and features.

❖ Working with the customer to verify that following the process and achieving the measures will in fact result in customer satisfaction.

The strategic quality plan addresses how we will use methods such as Design for Six Sigma (DFSS) to ensure a high level of customer and market focus. As discussed earlier, the Baldrige criteria provide strategic measures while Six Sigma provides tactical measures. The strategic quality plan describes how we are going to fuse these two levels to ensure that we "delight" the customer. An additional component of the strategic quality plan is the process of teaming with our customers and our suppliers to achieve a seamless process for excellence. This involves working together to improve the interactions between the three parties.

Strategic Regulatory Plan — The third leg in the integrated strategic plan includes the strategic regulatory plan. In the United States, for example, there are specific regulated industries such as those that fall under the Food and Drug Administration's regulation of food, drugs, cosmetics and medical devices; the Nuclear Regulatory Commission's regulation of nuclear energy; and the Securities Exchange Commission (stock transactions). There are many other companies, however, that don't think of themselves as being regulated but, in fact, are. In the United States, the Occupational Safety and Health Agency, the Environmental Protection Agency, the Department of Labor and the Internal Revenue Service, as well as many other state and local agencies, all require compliance with applicable regulations that impact departments like human resources, finance/accounting and legal.

These regulatory activities can cost us significant amounts of money and directly affect our bottom line. Some regulations are quite valuable and can help an organization improve its processes and act more responsibly — thereby improving the organization's image. Others may be the result of bureaucratic hairsplitting. Each area, however, has its own management system, and each system contains numerous opportunities for improvement. Moreover, since there are so many different management systems, there are plenty of opportunities to eliminate redundancies among the systems. Elimination of such redundancies can provide savings in cost, quality and cycle time. Integrated strategic planning is an essential part of what differentiates Fusion Management from other approaches, as we will see in the following chapter, which discusses the management of change.

5

Fusion Management and Change Management

When I meet with CEOs who insist that they want to make positive change, as in the case of the French company discussed earlier, I always ask the same question: How much of your personal time are you prepared to commit to leading the change process? The answer is, invariably, "Whatever it takes."

When I tell them that they will have to devote 40 hours a month to the process of achieving the new approach, I generally receive the same expressions of surprise, shock and dismay. It is difficult for them to accept that money and resources cannot be substituted for their personal time. As a result, only a small percentage of companies succeed in changing the way they do business. They are the ones that have CEOs who recognize the significance of this revision in personal style and attention. The key to accomplishing positive change is a CEO who truly comprehends the meaning of commitment. In this chapter, we will explain why change management is an essential component of Fusion Management.

COMPREHENSION BEFORE COMMITMENT

Consultants and business analysts who speak about performance excellence generally agree that "management commitment" is key to the ultimate success of the performance excellence process, and all performance excellence models have "leadership" or "management commitment" as a primary criterion. On the other hand, most executives are convinced that they indeed have always had a "performance excellence focus" and that the real need is for their subordinates to pay more attention to improving product or service quality.

This dichotomy of attitudes demonstrates a lack of comprehension on the part of the senior executives as to the true meaning of the performance excellence revolution. Executives need to understand their roles in the change process; they need to understand that what they do speaks louder than what they say.

For an organization to truly commit itself to the change process, its entire management team must be able to answer the following questions.

1. Why do you want to change?
2. What are the financial implications of change?
3. How will you measure the financial implications?
4. What do you expect the change to accomplish?
5. What do you need to alter to achieve change?
6. What are the barriers to change?
7. What can you do to overcome such barriers?
8. What resources does change require?
9. How will you acquire such resources?
10. What priorities should you set?
11. What process will you apply?

Each of these items is discussed below.

1. WHY CHANGE

One of the overriding motivations for change is competition. The globalization of markets has made it imperative for companies to continuously improve. It is no longer satisfactory for us to say that our performance, quality, productivity or cost is equal to or better than the rest of the industry. We must concentrate on how well we are satisfying the wants and needs of our customers and look for ways to exceed their expectations. This requires a better understanding of our customers and benchmarking against the best in class, regardless of industry.

Some definitions are required for clarification. Customer *needs* are the features of the product or service that satisfy some minimum requirement. A *want* is something that would be nice to have but is not usually included with this product or service. An *expectation* is usually something that the customer has received before or knows that other people have received before. A *delight* is some feature that you did not need or expect, but that makes the product more desirable — the product then exceeds your expectations.

Consider, for example, an automobile. You *need* a vehicle to get you from point A to point B reliably and efficiently. You may *want* an electronic navigational system, but if the system is not available on the model you like or is too expensive, you may be willing to settle for a digital compass. However, your *expectation* is undoubtedly that the car will have windshield wipers, because every car you have seen does, indeed, have them. If the car you get doesn't have windshield wipers, you will be very upset. But if it has windshield wipers that turn on automatically when it starts raining (and the car is running), you have a feature that exceeds your expectations — a feature may *delight* you. The next time you buy an automobile, automatic windshield wipers may be a *want*, or even an *expectation*.

Now if a competitor's automobile, in addition to everything else, has an electronic navigational system at the same price, customers will most likely switch to that vehicle. Customers are drawn to products that satisfy wants as well as needs. In fact, they may even switch to an auto that satisfies wants but costs more. Eventually, as we know, wants become needs and even expectations. Years ago, automatic transmission was a want for most drivers; today, it is a need (or even an expectation). Of course, there is a significant sector of the population that will pay extra, if required, to get a car with standard transmission. But who would buy a car that didn't have a radio?

The concept of benchmarking as a change management driver is another idea that many don't fully understand. Traditional thinking about benchmarking focuses on how we rate in our own industry against our traditional competitors. This thinking very often gives us a false sense of security; since we are operating at a high level compared to our traditional competition, there is no reason to improve. This complacency has enabled nontraditional competitors to overtake and surpass established providers, resulting in loss of market share and, in many cases, the demise of a profitable business.

The concept of benchmarking against the best in class leads us to look outside (as well as inside) our own industry or service sector to improve our business operations. For example, we can identify specific companies (irrespective of industry) that are the leaders in such activities as:

❖ Financial service.

❖ Customer service.

❖ Distribution.

❖ Human resources management.

❖ Information technology.

Since no one company is the best in every category, the approach is to learn from each company what it does best and how it does it. The objective of change is to improve until we match or exceed the best in each and every category.

2. FINANCIAL IMPLICATIONS OF CHANGE

We have asked thousands of senior executives from around the world, "What percent of your work day is spent on non-value-added activities?" These activities include time spent:

❖ Responding to a crisis.

❖ Recovering from a problem.

❖ Dealing with an irate customer.

❖ Following up on a supplier problem.

❖ Rereading an edited document (2nd, 3rd, 4th time).

❖ Attending a rerun of a meeting (2nd, 3rd, 4th time).

Although individual responses have ranged from as low as 10 percent to as high as 90 percent, the average is usually between 40 and 60 percent, indicating that executives spend about half their time on non-value-added activities. When we ask executives how much time their subordinates spend on these activities, the average is about the same, implying that about half of all management and administrative time is spent performing non-value-added activities.

If we extrapolate this (which is always risky), we can infer that we may have twice as many people, offices, desks, computers and phones as we need to do our jobs properly. The opportunity is clear, but frightening to contemplate. However, if our competitors deal with this non-value-added dilemma, their advantage will be significant.

How can we have allowed this level of waste to exist for so long? The answer is that the companies to which we compare ourselves are doing the same things as we do; therefore, there is no perceived incentive to improve. Unfortunately, there may very well be companies from other industries or other countries that are capable of taking our business away by providing better quality products and services at lower prices.

Recent exercises in so-called "downsizing" or "rightsizing" have been conducted in response to the excesses that have existed for decades. However, these painful cutbacks cause severe crises in many companies because they result in staff reductions without eliminating the source of the problem: excessive non-value-added efforts. In fact, downsizing arguably increases non-value-added costs — due to the extra responsibilities put on the remaining staff.

The key to financial improvement is to eliminate (or at least significantly reduce) sources of non-value-added activities and to focus resources on improving our products and services.

3. MEASURING THE FINANCIAL IMPLICATIONS OF CHANGE

Non-value-added time is responsible for a significant part of the cost of nonquality that all companies face. Most manufacturing companies equate product scrap costs with cost of nonquality; they completely ignore wasted time as a significant factor. In fact, many components of the cost of nonquality are strategically buried in the company's standard cost system. If 50 percent of a person's time is spent on non-value-added activities, then it takes two people, two desks, two computers, two telephones — literally two of everything — to do every job that one person should be able to do. Hence, finance has created a system that says, in effect, $2 = $1. Thus, as long as we spend approximately $2 on every task there is no perception that a problem exists. The standard says we should be spending $2, and the variance reports confirm that we are, indeed, spending $2. Unfortunately, as Juran would say, we have disconnected the alarm signals, so nobody takes any action.

Crises tend to manifest themselves when the system begins to cost some larger value, say $3 or more, rather than the anticipated $2. In these cases, most companies would view a return to the $2 cost as an improvement, but in reality it is only a return to the inefficient status quo of 2 = 1.

Improvement occurs as we reduce $2 to $1.50 to $1.25 to $1.10 and ultimately to $1. These concepts are illustrated in Figure 5-1.

If we look at Figure 5-1 we see that the $2 cost consists of a real cost of $1 and an extra non-value-added cost of $1 (a total of $2 for standard cost). As long as the cost stays close to $2 no action is taken. But when the cost reaches the threshold of pain (say $3), a crisis ensues and all of management descends on the affected area.

In a typical facility you can tell where the crisis is because management is huddled around the activity, person or machine with the problem. Sometimes you can even see them praying, "Please get better, please get better." Oftentimes, the problem goes away quite miraculously. Nobody knows why the problem occurred or why it went away, but they brush their brows in relief,

FIGURE 5-1 BUSINESS IMPROVEMENT CYCLE

System Evolution/Design	Product/System Verification	System Optimization	Breakthrough
The effort before the system is put in place to prevent failures by proper system design.	The effort after the system is put in place to detect deviations from the norm and return the process to that norm.	The effort to reduce the norm (chronic problems) to lower and lower levels until it finally approaches real cost.	The effort to get "out of the box." Achieving dramatic improvements in critical measures of performance.

System fully implemented

CRISIS

Threshold of pain

Non-value-added cost

Real cost

Lessons learned applied to future systems

thank heaven that all is well and return to their offices. Management meetings usually do nothing to improve processes or reduce non-value-added costs, but they represent a significant portion of a company's wasted time. Real system improvement takes place (as shown on the right-hand side of Figure 5-1) when the non-value-added costs are brought closer to zero.

The left-hand side of the figure refers to system evolution. In most companies management systems have simply evolved, with new procedures, practices and forms added to meet each new situation. In short, they have not been designed. Although we would like to believe that there is system design, the reality is that each person or group responsible for a subset of activities comprising an aspect of the system has customized a portion of the system to suit its particular needs. Usually, this is at the customer's expense — either their external customer (consumer, client) or their internal customer (the operators of the next step in the process). The process described in Figure 5-1 needs to be replaced with a system design and a control process to achieve excellence.

Many people believe that companies registering for ISO 9001 had to design effective processes and systems in order to be registered. However, our experience demonstrates that a substantial number of consultants and registrars encourage clients to document processes exactly as they are being performed to assure that the company passes the third-party assessment for ISO 9001:2000 registration.

"Documenting what you do" may be an expedient tactic for achieving registration, but it's clearly not effective for improving the quality or productivity of your organization. To explore this more fully, consider the typical activities of an assessor (auditor) who visits a facility for a few short days to evaluate the effectiveness of the quality system. A US regulatory agency's auditing body found the results shown in Figure 5-2 when it summarized the audit findings over an extended period. Clearly, 75 percent of the system audit findings, which are typical, are based on absences of procedures or people not following procedures.

❖ To determine whether or not a process is documented, one only has to ask, "Do you have a written procedure for this activity?" If the answer is yes, the next question is, "May I see it?" About 20 percent of findings result when, in fact, there is no procedure.

❖ If the auditor is shown the procedure, the next step is to determine if it is being followed. At this point, 55 percent of findings tend to be instances where the procedure is not being followed. By carefully following the procedure, an auditor will indeed find areas where personnel have changed the procedure to suit their own needs. It is precisely because these two areas are so easy to uncover in an audit that companies and consultants tend to opt for "documenting what's being done."

FIGURE 5-2 TYPICAL AUDIT RESULTS

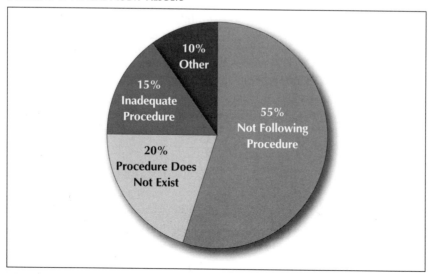

❖ The next question should be, "Is the procedure effective?" But this question is more difficult to assess. To demonstrate that failures occur, even when the procedure is being followed, is difficult. However, from the perspective of those who want to improve their company's performance, it is the most important question.

If, in fact, we opt to document the status quo, we have selected a path that suboptimizes our systems and legitimatizes excessive, non-value-added activities, as demonstrated in Figure 5-1.

Therefore, it is vital that we design our systems. This concept can be thought of as quality assurance, if that term is regarded in its broadest sense. Quality system designs are the products of:

❖ Extensive research into customer needs and wants.

❖ Efforts to convert customer needs and wants into a product or service concept.

❖ Establishing process and product specifications that, when met, result in a product or service that satisfies customer needs and wants.

❖ Efforts to reduce process variability to the degree that it exceeds customer expectations.

Returning to Figure 5-1, we see that the second segment is product and system verification. All forms of operations, whether related to manufacturing, service, or research and development, have a verification activity associated with them. By definition, verification is not a value-added activity. However, it may be necessary if quality performance is poor.

In this segment we see the process shifting from $2 to $3. These shifts are not uncommon, and every process has a threshold of pain, a point where attention must be paid. When this occurs management huddles and prays.

Occasionally, after the process has been returned to $2, someone states, "We were operating at $3 per unit; we are now at $2 per unit, and since we make a million of these a year, we have saved a million dollars per year." Unfortunately, at the end of the year, we don't see that money on the bottom line and we don't understand why. This type of crisis has the tendency to recur, and if it recurred once per month, we could claim a spurious $12 million in savings for the year.

This example is a case where a process went out of control and then returned (at least temporarily) to the apparently in-control state of $2 per unit cost. This is not continual improvement. This is verification and control.

Continual improvement is reflected in the third quadrant of Figure 5-1. Here, we make incremental improvements from $2 to $1.50 to $1.25 until we get to $1.00, the real cost. Even though we may not know the real cost, our process of continual improvement will move us toward the goal. Many people working on teams have asked me, "What will we do when we solve all of our problems?" The response takes us to the fourth quadrant of Figure 5-1 — "breakthrough." The real cost — $1.00 — is predicated on the specifics of our design. By "getting out of the box," by changing raw materials, service models, process flows, methodologies, etc., we may be able to achieve results representing order-of-magnitude returns. This figure also points out that we need to provide feedback on the improvements made in quadrants 2, 3 and 4 to ensure that the next version of the product or service benefits from what we have learned.

4. DEFINING EXPECTATIONS FOR CHANGE: THE INTEGRATED STRATEGIC PLAN

Most executives in the United States have been sufficiently bombarded over the past 10 to 15 years by newspaper and magazine articles and other literature about "quality." They understand the relationship between competitiveness and the quality of their products and services. European executives, on the other hand, are just beginning to hear the same message. Unfortunately, this message is being distorted worldwide. This distortion is very similar to static on the radio. In my opinion it is caused by an undue emphasis on the certification aspect of ISO 9001 rather than process improvement. As a result, management attention is focused not on the basic tenets of performance excellence, but rather the pursuit of a certificate.

Unfortunately, as mentioned earlier, many consultants and registrars encourage clients to document what they already do. Companies that want to improve quality need to employ a more robust approach; they have to commit to studying their system and improving upon it before proceeding to documentation. As noted in a recent *ISO Survey of ISO 9000 and ISO 14000 Certificates, Eleventh Cycle* by the International Organization for Standardization, there were 66,760 ISO 9000 certificates in the United Kingdom alone. In the United States there were 37,026 certificates contributing to a worldwide total of 510,616 as of December 2001. Among the certificate holders were colleges, law firms, health care providers and financial service organizations.

Several years ago there was a widely circulated story regarding a Malcolm Baldrige National Quality Award winner that had barely been able to achieve certification to ISO 9000. One would only hope that a high quality company would automatically qualify for compliance with a minimalist standard such as ISO 9000.

(Do not misinterpret our use of the word "minimalist;" we do not use it in a pejorative sense. As discussed earlier, consensus standards, by their very nature, embody compromise. Consensus requires extensive hours, months and years of discussion to achieve meaningful results that address the issues of all materially concerned parties. The end result represents a minimum requirement and not necessarily an optimum system.)

This leads us to consider what changes we should be expecting. The first major change required, as described in Chapter 4, is to develop a strategic quality plan that is integrated with the corporate strategic business plan and strategic regulatory plan. Most large companies and many smaller companies have a strategic business plan, but have yet to treat quality as a strategic initiative. In today's global economy, quality may be the most important strategy in any company's long-range plans.

Strategic business plans typically start with a definition of the company's vision. What does the company want to be in 5 or 10 years? All actions can then be assessed against the agreed-upon vision. The question that one needs to ask of all managerial decisions is, "Is this action going to move us in the direction of our vision (i.e., will it help us achieve our vision)?" If a decision will not move us in the proper direction, why would we make it?

The process of creating and agreeing on a vision statement usually takes a fair amount of effort. Once it is in place, it must be used as a guide for decision making. Recall from Chapter 1 how the brothers of the family-owned business recognized that the acquisition they were contemplating was not consistent with their strategic plan.

Another part of the strategic planning process is the mission statement. Many organizations confuse vision with mission. In fact, many organizations publish:

"VISION: Our mission is…"

Typically, each functional area (for example, engineering, production, finance or human resources) creates a mission statement to define what it does to help the company achieve its vision. If done properly, achieving the departmental missions will lead to attaining the company's vision. Within each department, sections define goals that are designed to aid the department in accomplishing its mission. For example, in the finance department, sections such as accounts receivable, accounts payable and payroll have established goals. Each individual then has specific objectives to aid the section in reaching its goals.

This concept is not new and many companies prepare their strategic business plans in this manner. Unfortunately, many companies expend significant effort and money to create a strategic business plan, but rarely use it to guide their decision-making processes. At best, they use the plan as an annual scorecard to determine how well they are doing. If they find they are not doing well against the plan, they decry the external, uncontrollable factors, such as a bad economy, unexpected competition, price increases and other factors, for their failures. They then tend to rationalize their current status and begin to predict that things will be different next year.

A strategic plan and a vision are only valuable if they are used as a set of parameters for managerial decision making. The plan needs to be a living document that is always in view and used as a set of guiding principles.

One of the items poorly addressed in most strategic business plans is quality. Typically, words like "acceptable quality" are included as part of a list of items that must be accomplished, but "acceptable" is generally not defined, nor is the process for specifying and achieving quality. Partially, this is due to a vague and ill-defined notion of quality.

Fusing an organization's quality plan with its strategic business plan enables it to use the excellence of its product or service to capture market. This approach requires an organization to identify its customer needs and wants and to devise a means for measuring satisfaction. Many organizations mistakenly use customer complaints as the metric for satisfaction, but this measure captures only the dissatisfaction of unhappy customers — leaving out the voices of satisfied customers, customers of competitors and noncustomers.

Once these needs and wants are identified, they must be translated into product features and then into specifications. This part of the process is called quality of design. For example, a bank planning a small business loan service may decide that farms and small shops have differing needs — that farms may need large sums at certain times of the year, while merchants need revolving lines of credit. As a result they must design different loan services for different customers. Some of the tools used to help us identify our customers and their needs and wants are benchmarking, voice of the customer, quality function deployment (QFD) and failure mode and effects analysis (FMEA). (In the Six Sigma process, as we have noted, these tools are collectively referred to as Design for Six Sigma–DFSS.)

Furthermore, we need to address the effect on process or product variation (or lack thereof) in regard to what the change will accomplish. Many organizations fail to appreciate the significance of consistency (minimum variation).

If you get paid on the 25th of the month, you expect that payment to be on time, every time. Planning your life — purchases, rent payments, bills and so on — would be difficult if your monthly paycheck appeared on a randomly selected day each month. Most employees will tell you, "I don't care which day of the month I get paid on as long as it is the same day each month. That's the only way I can plan my expenditures."

An effective strategic business plan examines what an organization does well and what it does not do well. It compares an organization's performance to that of its competitors and other unrelated companies; it examines the barriers that prevent an organization from adhering to financial goals. The strategic quality plan examines (through benchmarking) how the best in class operates and uses this knowledge to raise the organization's performance in all aspects of business operations to the level of world-class performance. This fusion quality-centered approach ultimately leads to achieving or surpassing the goals of the strategic business plan.

The third strategic component is the strategic regulatory plan. As discussed in Chapter 4, many US executives, when asked if their companies are regulated, say "no" because they think of regulated as controlled by requirements of agencies such as FDA (Food and Drug Administration), FCC (Federal Communications Commission) or FAA (Federal Aviation Administration). Virtually all companies, however, are regulated by organizations and laws, for example, the IRS (Internal Revenue Service), SEC (Securities and Exchange Commission), EPA (Environmental Protection Agency), OSHA (Occupational Safety and Health Agency) and FLSA (Fair Labor Standards Act) in the case of US companies. A disregard of these requirements could easily result in plant closings and/or significant fines and incarceration.

Fusing business, quality and regulatory plans makes a great deal of practical sense for any organization that wants to optimize its business processes (see Figure 4-7, page 106).

5. WHAT NEEDS TO CHANGE

Leadership's Management Style – In Chapter 1 we stressed leadership as an essential difference in Fusion Management. In order to effect change, company leaders must focus on understanding and satisfying customers. The key is to exceed customer expectations. The leadership of an organization must serve as the agent of change; leaders need to change their style from managerial control to true leadership. For the most part, our business schools have emphasized only the control aspects of management. Fusion Management leaders have to

Figure 5-3 Required Changes in Management Style

From Managing By	To Leading By
Planning	Mentoring
Controlling	Coaching, Guiding, Facilitating
Giving Orders	Setting an Example
Instinct (Experience)	Fact (Information)
Crisis	Consistent Behavior

be mentors, coaches, facilitators and guides. Figure 5-3 demonstrates some of the differences between traditional management styles and the leadership that is now required.

Leadership can transcend the gap between labor and management. A number of organizations have created leadership teams comprised of executives and union leaders.

Information — The second required change concerns the manner in which information is created and used. Many organizations claim to have insufficient data, but in reality they usually have an overwhelming amount of data (often far more than they need) — what they lack is information. Information, as we have explained, can only be gained through analyzing data in such a way as to enable management and others to make informed decisions.

Often, companies move from crisis to crisis and never have time to plan, organize, investigate, analyze, interpret, assess and act. We know about Shewhart's "plan-do-study-act" cycle. Unfortunately, most organizations proceed immediately to "act." Many actually measure progress by motion, forming special "task forces" to cope with sudden changes. If enough people are running around frantically, the assumption is that something positive is being accomplished. This assumption is usually incorrect.

Modern organizations recognize that they need to train people to use information more effectively. However, many people don't understand the distinction between data and information, so they train too many personnel in quantitative techniques such as basic statistics.

It isn't unusual for us to receive requests from companies looking for training in advanced statistical process control (SPC). They inform us that during the past year they have trained all 200 (or 5,000) employees in SPC, and although everyone knows how to plot control charts, they don't know how to interpret them. Either the training wasn't effective or it wasn't properly applied — if people do not apply what they are taught, they forget what they learn.

One of the difficulties is the emphasis on training rather than on education. Training is typically aimed at teaching a skill that can be applied to a given set of conditions. Education, on the other hand, aims to provide a knowledge base, perhaps in the form of a number of models that can be drawn upon to assess a set of conditions.

Most people associate practice (experience) with skill development (training) but not with education. It is our contention that education is not completed until an individual has applied the processes that he or she has been exposed to, at least two or three times. Behavior modification (change) takes place after people have had several successes in applying a new process; only then does the new process become equally or more comfortable to use than the previous process.

Consider, for example, a situation common in many large and medium-size companies. Many members of the management team have experience and training in problem-solving techniques, team building and other approaches. However, when members of such a group are presented with a problem to solve, they generally work by themselves (rather than in a team) using a trial and error approach rather than relying on the techniques they have been taught. If this is true for all of the other training they have been through, why should anyone expect a new style of training to be any more effective? This is why we emphasize that the change process can only occur in information-driven organizations that make decisions based on facts. For this to happen, senior executives have to insist that subordinates employ an information-driven approach. They need to ensure that decisions are supported by facts and are designed to deal with root-cause issues — not just symptoms.

Many organizations spend a great deal of time "solving" the same problem over and over again. Clearly, they are unable to get to the root cause of the problem. Again, this is an example of a great deal of non-value-added time being spent.

If the executive staff is going to lead an organization into managing by fact, they have to do it as well. The executive committee has to become personally proficient in assessing information and insist that their staff only present proposals that are supported by analysis, interpretation and assessment.

Another aspect of information is the ability to demonstrate that improvement efforts are indeed resulting in changes that contribute to the goals of a company's strategic plan. Key to success is having a strategic quality plan and strategic regulatory plans that fully support the strategic business plan. Organizations must possess the ability to quantify and demonstrate the relationship between actions and business results. This is where Six Sigma has made such a significant breakthrough — personnel trained as black belts generally undergo four weeks of training over 16 weeks, with 12 of the weeks focused on completing at least one project with verified and validated business results (see Chapter 6).

Fusion Management addresses many of the deficiencies described above. It focuses on training the senior executive team (SET) to become the mentors, coaches and champions that lead an organization in deploying the Six Sigma approach. The SET selects candidates for Six Sigma black belt training, organizes the selection of projects, ensures that barriers are removed, reviews the application of the process and the results and validates that the business results are real. Furthermore, the company's future leadership will be comprised of those who are most successful in applying the process that Fusion Management embraces.

Human Resources — Effectively developing and managing human resources is another area that requires substantial attention. The plan and implementation for this process have to be designed so that they, too, support the strategic quality plan, the strategic regulatory plan and the strategic business plan (SBP). This means that a company's reward and recognition process as well as its education and training process have to be consistent with the SBP.

The traditional organization tries to reward individual efforts and accomplishments. The evolved organization must realize that if it is requesting people to work in teams, then it must issue rewards and recognition to teams as well as to individuals. It does not help morale or participation to see an individual performance appraisal such as this:

"We really appreciate the great accomplishments you have made, with your process improvement team reporting a $450,000 annual savings. But you failed to accomplish two of your personal objectives for the year so your salary increase has been reduced."

Clearly this approach sends the message that even though management says they want you to work on teams, they don't really value team activity.

Rewards and recognition present other difficulties as well. Frederick Herzberg, in his comparison of satisfiers and dissatisfiers, points out that salary, supervision, company policy and working conditions are much more likely to dissatisfy than to satisfy. The satisfiers tend to be achievement, recognition, the work itself, responsibility and advancement (with the last three having the greatest long-term effect). When most people hear that money is more of a dissatisfier than a satisfier, they are surprised. The following example explains this premise. If you are expecting a 5 percent salary increase and receive 5 percent, it does nothing to satisfy you since you discounted its value long ago. If, on the other hand, someone in your group receives 6 percent, or you only receive 4 percent, you would probably be very dissatisfied. However, if you received 6 percent and others did not, you would probably be pleased; but usually that satisfaction only lasts a short time. Figure 5-4 shows Herzberg's representation of satisfiers and dissatisfiers and their impact.

Process Management — Management must change its mode of operation from crisis management to a systematic series of processes aimed at achieving ever-higher quality and performance excellence. Perhaps one of the most

FIGURE 5-4 THE MANAGER AND THE HUMAN SCIENCES

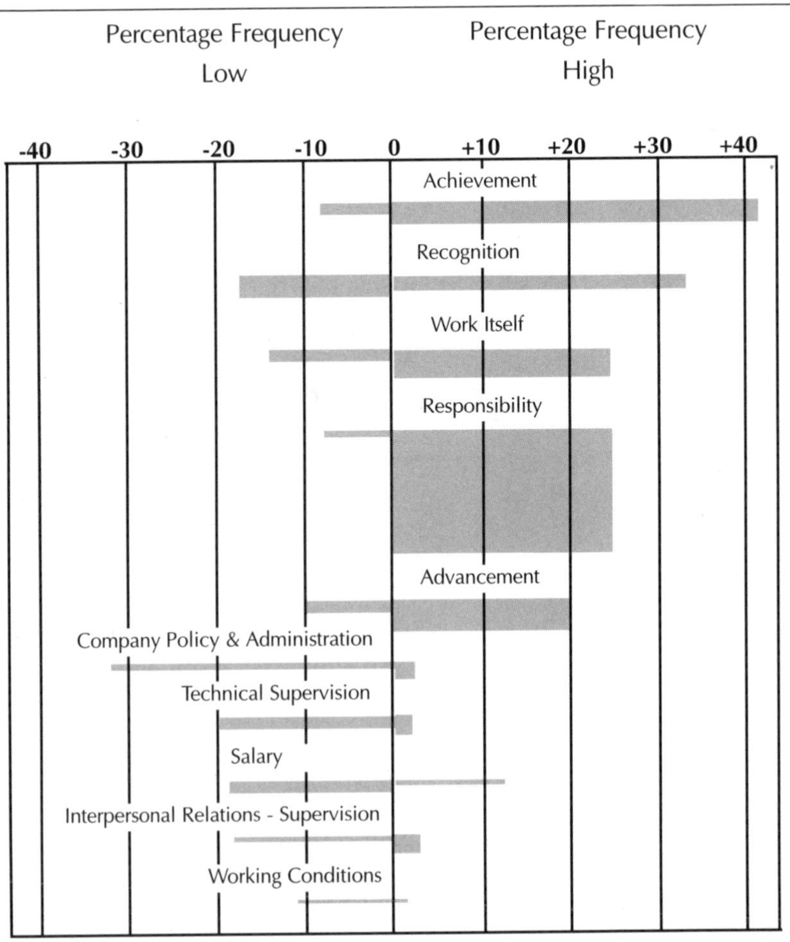

Note: The length of the grey areas represents the frequency of occurrence; the thickness represents the duration of effects.

important concerns of any company is how new and improved products and services are designed and introduced.

In many companies the concept of "over the fence design" has become the norm. Designers work on the service or product design until time runs out and then turn it over to operations to make it work. Typically, no attention is paid to designing the processes for producing, distributing and providing after-sale service for the product. This often results in months of poor service to customers and loss of market due to damaged company image.

Many people were surprised when Cadillac Motor Company won the Malcolm Baldrige National Quality Award in 1990 since Cadillac's reputation had been in decline. Many people even voiced concern over the credibility of the Baldrige Award. However, Cadillac had demonstrated to the Baldrige Board of Examiners that, among other things, it had successfully implemented a concurrent engineering process. The process made sure that everyone in the product chain actively participated in the quality process, which involved all of the operations from concept to delivery, service and end user feedback. The validity of that process was demonstrated in 1992 when the new Cadillac Seville, the first product of this concurrent engineering process, won the following awards: *Motor Week* Driver's Choice, *Car and Driver*'s Ten Best, *Motor Trend* Car of the Year and *Popular Mechanics* Award for Design and Engineering.

When most people think of process quality, their minds immediately focus on "product." Over the years, we have become conditioned to correlate quality with the acceptability or performance characteristics of the end (hardware) product. In today's global economy, customer satisfaction is determined at least as often by service as it is by the product itself.

As discussed earlier, Shewhart in his 1931 text *Economic Control of Quality of Manufactured Product* defined quality as:

❖ Satisfying human wants through the fabrication of raw materials into finished product.

   - The first step is for the engineer to translate these wants into physical characteristics.

   - The second step is for the engineer to reduce the variability of the process.

In other words, Shewhart had codified, prior to 1931, virtually all of the quality concepts that we discuss today as "new." Figure 5-5 compares Shewhart's view in 1931 to some of the key issues today.

Figure 5-5 Quality Emphasis

Shewhart (1931)	Fusion Management
❖ Define what the customer wants	❖ Listen to the voice of the customer
❖ Translate wants into physical characteristics	❖ Use quality function deployment (QFD)
❖ Continually shift standards depending on shifting human wants	❖ Continual improvement
❖ Develop process to meet requirements	❖ Reduced variation (i.e., Taguchi methods) ❖ Process management ❖ Concurrent engineering

Unfortunately, quality control and quality assurance, as practiced in the past, were often driven by a management style that either refused to listen to those who understood the broader concepts of performance excellence or had very little regard for the contribution that could be provided by a proper quality approach. Hence, they frequently fulfilled their own expectations by dumping the least qualified engineers into the quality role, assuring that the organization wouldn't get much useful advice from this part of the company.

The evolved organization looks at its processes with the aim of designing its systems to satisfy both needs and wants, as discussed previously, and focuses on achieving the Fusion Management perspective. In this approach, process management has very significant implications for the business processes and support services. A concerted effort needs to be applied to improve quality, performance and cycle time. Not only do customers expect products to perform as advertised, but they expect to be treated in a courteous and efficient way. The days are gone, in most cases, where the customer has no other choice but to buy it or live without it. Today, the competition is serious.

6. Barriers to Change

Companies that do not become information-driven and customer-focused risk extinction. Results need to demonstrate that we have designed, developed and implemented a strategy that satisfies customers and demonstrates measurable improvements in the quality of service, product, business process, support service and suppliers. We must be able to quantitatively show that we are satisfying customers. Furthermore, there should be clear evidence that these measurable improvements have resulted in advances in productivity, efficiency and effectiveness that provide bottom-line results in the company's financial and operational metrics.

7. OVERCOMING BARRIERS TO CHANGE

The predominant barrier to change is the resistance of personnel. Interestingly, the resistance is most commonly found at the supervisory and management levels, not at the operator level. It is common to hear operational people identify their management as not understanding what is going on in the company and behaving in ways that prevent service and product quality from being the best it can be.

Many supervisors and managers (as well as senior executives) were raised in environments that emphasized control. As a result, the predominant managerial philosophy states that people will slow down, make bad quality or provide mediocre service if they are not closely supervised. Yet this same management group agrees that they and their subordinates spend 50 percent of their time in non-value-added activities. Often, change doesn't even occur in companies where senior executives are well aware of the benefits that would come along with it. This is because middle managers, staff and supervisors are uncomfortable with change. In fact, fear of giving up control is a real obstacle for many people.

Many workers don't believe that management will change. Over the years managers have made many aborted attempts at such management "fads" as cost reduction, profit improvement, management by objectives, participative management, zero defects and quality circles. Eventually, each of these *programmes du jour* met its demise because management lacked a true consistency of purpose. Employees hearing of any new scheme are convinced that management will not maintain the process.

I have frequently visited companies that are trying to introduce a new program, only to find the operational personnel wagering a dollar apiece in a pool that will be paid to the individual who comes closest to guessing when the program will die. One of the primary reasons for the frailty of these quality initiatives is a lack of management comprehension before commitment. This typically leads to management's trying to measure success in ways that ultimately doom the initiative.

In the 1950s, as we have seen, managers measured the success of their SPC activities by counting how many control charts were in place in their company. In many cases, companies ended up with "the great control chart race," resulting in charts being implemented strictly to increase the count — without adding any value to the processes being charted. Eventually, all of these charts were discarded.

In the 1970s, as another example, quality circles were widely introduced in North and South American companies. Again, managers measured success in terms of the number of quality circle teams they formed. Circles eventually disbanded because:

- ❖ Middle managers and supervisors felt threatened by the activities of teams that were created by senior executives and made up of operational personnel.
- ❖ Measuring success in terms of the number of teams in place resulted in the institutionalization of teams and the discrediting of their work.

In the 1980s and 1990s, many companies embraced total quality management (TQM). In many cases, however, companies were emphasizing form rather than substance and were counting the number of SPC charts and problem-solving teams that had been put in place.

Perhaps the greatest barrier to change, however, is our perception of self and others. As long as we perceive that we're okay and everyone else needs to change, little progress can be made. A well-known CEO of a Baldrige award-winning company explained that a major turnaround in his organization occurred when he recognized that managers, not operators, were responsible for quality problems. He made the realization at a company banquet, and when he did, he stood up on a chair and prophetically told his executives that if they were to change and improve, they all needed to get up and acknowledge, "We are the problem."

The best way for a company to overcome most of these barriers to change is to have a clear focus on the customer. This includes internal as well as external customers. The process of creating the strategic quality plan produces a clear definition of vision, mission(s), goals, objectives, strategies and tactics. It enables an organization to answer the following questions.

- ❖ Who are our customers?
- ❖ What are their needs and wants?
- ❖ How do we measure those needs and wants?
- ❖ How well are we satisfying those needs and wants?
- ❖ What can we do to exceed customer expectations?

This approach gives each part of an organization the ability to concentrate on accomplishing a series of supportive activities that together will result in the company's realization of its vision.

8. IDENTIFYING THE REQUIRED RESOURCES

Most organizations say, "If only we had 'X,' our problems would go away." That 'X' is usually something that has been requested before and has been turned down for lack of capital funds. Many of these people fail to recognize that there are two distinct forms of potential improvement. One form is usually referred to as breakthrough or innovation; it generally involves infusions of capital investment and the application of sophisticated analytical tools. The second, usually referred to as continual improvement, is made up of small, incremental changes that do not generally require large financial investments or advanced technology. The entire organization can contribute very specifically to continual improvement projects. Since the majority of opportunities for improvement are management controllable, not operator controllable (that is, the systems, not the people, are the source of the problem), executives and managers must invest their personal time to lead system improvement initiatives.

As we have stated repeatedly, it is generally easier for the executive committee to invest money rather than personal time, yet it is their personal time that makes the greatest short-term impact on improving quality, productivity and profitability.

The major investment required is in focusing executive, management, supervisory and staff time on the corporate systems that represent the greatest opportunities for improvement. This time resource needs to be applied first, to learning how to make the changes discussed earlier and second, to learning how to employ quantitative and qualitative management skills for information-driven decision processes.

Some organizations assume that if they have the will to make the change, it can be done. That is not always true. Often, the services of a third party, with the knowledge and ability to guide the executive committee's use of new management skills, will make a significant difference in how successful the organization ultimately will become. The outsider has the advantage of being able to concentrate on specific problems or issues. This is where Six Sigma enters the picture — with champions, master black belts, black belts and green belts focusing on achieving 10x returns on specific projects.

The most highly evolved companies are those that have educated senior executives in the change process. Educated executives drive change through an organization. Cascading from level to level, the process ultimately involves everyone in the company.

9. ASSESSING EXISTING RESOURCES

The first step is to perform a comprehensive and objective assessment of what resources exist and their effectiveness. Throughout this chapter we have shown that many of the purported resources and processes that companies put in place don't really serve a useful function. For example:

❖ Strategic business plans that are locked up where nobody can read them.

❖ Control charts that don't control anything.

❖ Internal audits that don't check anything beyond how carefully documented procedures are being followed.

❖ Procedures that require multiple signatures when only one person actually checks the process.

An in-depth assessment will identify what is serving a useful function and what is not. Part of this assessment should include flowcharts of the overall process — flowcharts will identify the biggest opportunities for improvement.

The evaluation of existing resource processes requires that an inventory be taken of personnel that have been trained in previous *programmes du jour*. How many of these personnel are actually applying what they were taught in the past? My experience is that if we have trained about 20 people, we can probably find one or two who are using what was presented. In many cases these individuals would make good candidates for participation in, or leadership of, the Fusion Management approach. Their use of learned skills makes them natural team leaders (officially or unofficially). In some cases they are at a lower level of management than others on the team, but they are always highly respected, which shows when higher levels of management defer to their skills and capabilities. The way in which we identify available resources must be analyzed to make sure that it corresponds to the goals of the strategic plan. If it does, we can be sure that we are investing our resources where they are most likely to move us in the direction of achieving our vision.

10. SETTING PRIORITIES

Identifying priorities in a logical manner comes from locating the greatest opportunities for improvement and focusing on them. A strategic quality plan helps an organization set appropriate priorities by clearly defining the outcomes that should be valued in terms of increasing customer satisfaction, improving profits, reducing cycle times, lowering costs and growing and developing the personnel and the organization. In short, our priorities should yield benefits to all of our stakeholders, including the community.

11. CUSTOMIZING THE PROCESS

The process of becoming a world-class competitor will vary. The process has to consider the basic culture or cultures that impact an organization. Today, given the global economy and the international nature of movies, television, music, the Internet and consumer products, many cultural aspects of perception are universal, but others are still national, regional and local. Typically, there are several cultures that need to be considered.

Corporate Cultures — In IBM, GE, Panasonic or American Express, there are certain corporate rules to be followed and ways of getting things done, regardless of whether the facility is located in New York, California, Paris or Tokyo.

Occupational Cultures — Engineers, software designers, scientists, electricians, carpenters, accountants and so forth often use common vocabularies, employ the same tools, follow similar procedures and generally feel most comfortable with others who understand their skills and problems.

Ethnic/National Cultures — Panasonic USA does many things differently from Panasonic Japan or Europe because the national (or even regional) cultures are different. Within the United States, a plant with a large minority or ethnically diverse work force may have different communication problems, serve different foods in their cafeterias and have work rules that accommodate certain ethnic customs.

Facility Cultures — Most large, multinational conglomerates grew partly by acquiring smaller, well-established firms. Although there may be attempts to impose certain corporatewide processes on the acquired entity (for example, financial reporting), the successful entity has its own facility culture. "In this plant, we always do it this way" and under most circumstances, management will not tamper with it.

The resultant approach incorporates all the components of the change process discussed earlier. It sets forth a continual improvement process designed to produce short-term improvements while simultaneously creating a solid foundation and a constancy of purpose. It will imbue quality improvement into all the routine activities performed throughout the organization. It will focus attention on 10x (order of magnitude) returns. Then, through the application of Fusion Management, the company will be on its way to world-class status and performance excellence.

We have fused the best aspects of all of the various quality techniques and programs into one six-step model for introducing Fusion Management into an organization.

6

A Model for Implementing Fusion Management

Fusion Management is about bringing together the finest aspects of a variety of management systems. It can provide your company with a unique, customized management system that incorporates only the appropriate aspects of Six Sigma, performance excellence and every other initiative that exists or has existed within your enterprise. It involves studying each enterprise, business unit, division and facility and then molding an overall approach that all stakeholders can embrace and that each enterprise can use to drive business results to previously unattainable levels of success.

Fusion Management is the product of lessons learned from the extensive array of *programmes du jour* that have come and (perhaps) gone. We have analyzed their philosophies, approaches, tools, methods, insights, successes, failures and information and created out of that analysis a *fused approach* that best fits the needs, wants, expectations, culture, prior experiences and future strategic objectives of your organization. Before we describe our implementation model, let's briefly review the origins of the Fusion Management concept.

THE EVOLUTION OF FUSION MANAGEMENT

We have referred to Fusion Management as the process of selecting the best features of many management approaches, building on their incremental successes and focusing on the continual enhancement of these efforts.

In recent years, there has been considerable talk about integrated management systems. Often, the discussion centers on integrating, as a minimum, a quality management system (usually ISO 9001 based) with an environmental management system (usually ISO 14001 based). This integration is now relatively simple because the ISO technical committees that created these standards have embarked on a joint effort to ensure that the two systems complement one another.

Some people believe that an integrated management system should also include health and safety management systems (such as OHSAS 18001) or social accountability systems (such as SA 8000). We can think of the first phase of integrated management systems as the *interrelationship* between quality, environmental and health and safety management systems (Figure 6-1).

Figure 6-1 Typical Integrated Management System

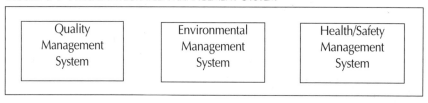

However, as we continue our investigation into related management systems, we find examples of systems designed to meet industry, sector-specific or regulatory requirements.

- ❖ ISO/TS 16949 — ISO 9001 plus automotive add-ons.
- ❖ TL 9000 — ISO 9001 plus telecommunication add-ons.
- ❖ AS9100 — ISO 9001 plus aerospace add-ons.
- ❖ TickIT — ISO 9001 plus software-specific requirements.
- ❖ 21 CFR 820 — FDA Quality System Regulation plus ISO 9001 plus medical device add-ons.
- ❖ ISO 13485 — ISO 9001 plus medical device requirements.
- ❖ Other — Various other regulatory requirements — EPA, EU requirements, CE marking, etc.

The result of implementing these requirements and specifications is an integrated management system that includes sector-specific and regulatory requirements (Figure 6-2).

In addition to the management systems listed above, unique enterprise-wide management systems exist for a wide scope of industries.

Figure 6-2 Integrated Management System Including Sector-Specific and Regulatory requirements

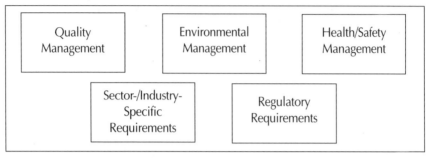

- ❖ Financial.
- ❖ Human resources.
- ❖ Engineering.
- ❖ Research, design and development.
- ❖ Operations.
- ❖ Purchasing and materials.
- ❖ Production.
- ❖ Storage and distribution.
- ❖ Administration.

Figure 6-3 is an expanded diagram of what an integrated management system would address.

If we integrate management systems of all types with Six Sigma/breakthrough management tools and performance excellence models, we have a model for Fusion Management, as shown in Figure 6-4. As of now, these three systems offer the best tools for improving the efficiency and effectiveness of your organization. When used in combination, within the Fusion Management system, they offer unparalleled results.

The following model described in this chapter has evolved over the past 40-plus years. It is a robust process that enables each enterprise to apply an approach to understanding its current business model ("as-is"), defining where it wants to be ("should-be"), making (incremental) improvements to achieve the "should-be state," defining stretch goals (integrated strategic plans), creating and deploying a master plan (managerial breakthrough), cascading the process throughout the enterprise and achieving highly successful business results.

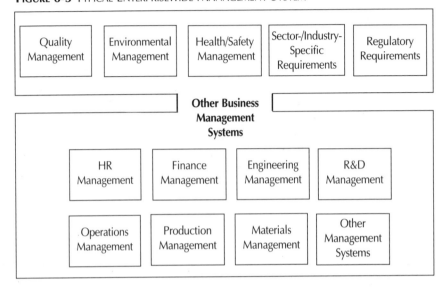

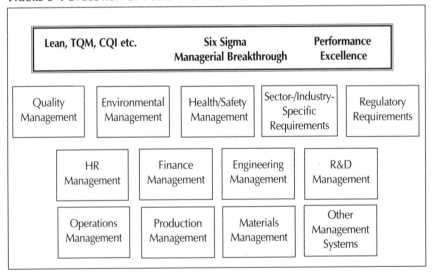

Six Steps to Fusion Management

The organization that is ready for Fusion Management already has a functioning quality management system (ISO 9001 or equivalent) or is in the process of documenting one, meets a high percentage of the applicable regulatory requirements and is seriously considering or is already involved in Lean,

TQM, Six Sigma or a similar business improvement process. A functioning documented quality management system, which includes internal audits, management reviews and effective preventive and corrective action processes, is essential as the foundation for any sophisticated business improvement process. In our implementation model, we assume that a documented quality management system is in place and will be upgraded or modified as necessary to accommodate new and changing requirements. Having said that, we have worked with organizations that have successfully implemented a basic management system (such as ISO 9001) in tandem with advanced concepts like Six Sigma (see Chapter 3 — The Wheelock Story).

The Fusion Management Implementation Model (shown in Figure 6-5) is a phased, logical approach that assures that your business, quality, performance and regulatory initiatives are merged. We recommend that an organization always begin with step one of the six-step implementation model, which defines the "as-is" condition of the organization, develops the foundation for implementing Fusion Management and firmly establishes the senior executive process as an ongoing element of the operation. As shown in Figure 6-6, several of the steps are implemented in parallel and all of them are ongoing activities.

FIGURE 6-5 THE FUSION MANAGEMENT IMPLEMENTATION MODEL

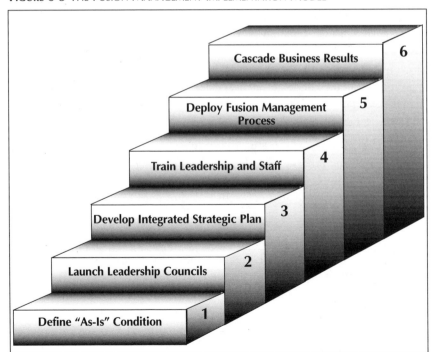

FIGURE **6-6** TIME LINE FOR IMPLEMENTATION OF FUSION MANAGEMENT

Time Line
Step
1 — Define "As-Is" Condition
2 — Launch Leadership Councils
3 — Develop Integrated Strategic Plan
4 — Train Leadership and Staff
5 — Deploy Fusion Management Process
6 — Cascade Business Results
Ongoing Fusion Management Practices

The Fusion Management Business Process Improvement model balances enterprisewide change management with quantitative analytical methods and tools. The results are improved managerial performance and unprecedented levels of business results.

Figure 6-7, a more detailed expansion of the six core Fusion Management steps, includes the senior executive process, which is the methodology we use to keep leadership involved. The details of the process are described in the remainder of this chapter, as well as in the accompanying charts. For example, assessing the "as-is" situation encompasses activities 1.1 through 1.7 of the more detailed flowchart in Figure 6-7, and these activities are an expansion of step one. Analyzing the "as-is" situation at an organization involves identifying the relevant methodologies in use, determining how well they are deployed and assessing how effectively they are integrated into the organization's overall business management system.

This "as-is" assessment defines the existing business processes, management systems and process controls. The resulting short-term plan outlines the steps necessary for deploying Fusion Management throughout the organization and includes measurable goals, objectives and responsibilities, as well as a target time line.

By performing the basic business analyses described in step one, the organization is able to recognize initial opportunities for improvement by reducing cycle time, eliminating redundancies and removing non-value-added activities. This approach highlights prime opportunities for breakthrough improvements.

FIGURE 6-7 THE DETAILED FUSION MANAGEMENT IMPLEMENTATION PROCESS

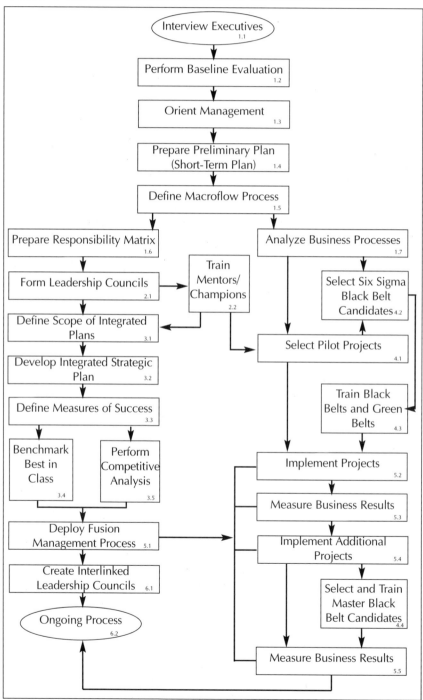

Step One: Define the "As-Is" Condition — the Senior Executive Process™

In this process, shown in Figure 6-8, management establishes the initial framework for the Fusion Management implementation plan shown in Figure 6-7. (The senior executive team then remains involved in the entire senior executive process.) Hence, when mentor training takes place as part of step two, the organization's hierarchy is prepared to incorporate the training results into its operations. Fusion Management employs such practices in order to effectively lower costs, remove non-value-added steps from operations, reduce cycle times, make breakthrough (order-of-magnitude) improvements and improve profits.

The organization can tailor a process that starts with understanding the strengths, weaknesses, opportunities and threats to the enterprise. It focuses on the mind-set of each member of the senior executive team, as well as on the mind-set of the team as a whole. The business assets (personnel, product, process, performance) are analyzed to define the baseline of current results and the use of modern methods and tools for business improvement. This baseline evaluation and planning session, described in Section 1.2, is an essential component of the senior executive process described below.

(Note: The numbers below in parentheses correspond to the numbered activities on Figures 6-7 through 6-12.)

(1.1) Interview Executives — The process facilitator (who may be an internal or external consultant, but who should be capable of evaluating the organization objectively) begins by becoming acquainted with the organization's operations. During this time, key executives and functional managers are interviewed while available business plans and top-level quality and regulatory plans are reviewed. The purpose of this effort is to address such questions as:

- ❖ What is the general understanding of the concepts of Fusion Management, Six Sigma, Lean, TQM, continual improvement, managerial breakthrough and performance excellence?

- ❖ What is the degree of senior management understanding of and commitment to this Fusion Management initiative?

- ❖ What management systems and process improvement tools or other activities are currently in place? How effectively are they operating?

- ❖ With which previous or current quality/excellence initiatives has the enterprise been involved?

- ❖ Is there any resistance (or reluctance) to pursuing the Fusion Management objectives?

FIGURE 6-8 STEP ONE: DEFINE "AS-IS" CONDITION

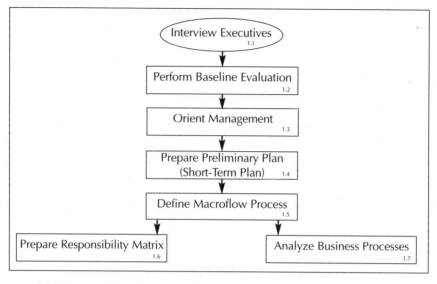

❖ What are the primary market, customer, competitive or internal forces pressing for a Fusion Management approach?

❖ Are there any preconceived expectations of the Fusion Management implementation?

❖ What is the facilitator's expected role?

❖ Are the right people scheduled to attend the planning session?

(1.2) Perform Baseline Evaluation (Gap Analysis) — The baseline evaluation team conducts a "walk-through" of the facility. Business assets (personnel-product-process-performance) are analyzed to prepare the current performance baseline and to determine the extent to which business improvement methods and tools are being used. When the team visits a department, the department head or functional area manager participates in the evaluation. This approach enables an organization to conduct a "gap analysis," which will determine exactly what methods and process improvement tools Fusion Management has to offer the department.

(1.3) Orient Management — This orientation enables the executive staff to understand the "what" and "how" of Fusion Management and to assess what role Fusion Management can play in achieving the enterprise's strategic objectives. The program content describes how Fusion Management objectives can be attained by all employees, including those indirectly involved in designing, producing and delivering products and services. Fusion Management teams are defined, performance measurements are identified and continuous improvement and breakthrough tools are introduced. Finally, the concepts are brought together to fit into the Fusion Management process model.

(1.4) Prepare Short-Term Fusion Plan — The Senior Executive Team compiles and reports on baseline evaluation results. Based on this report and the information obtained during the baseline evaluation, the group develops a *short-term* action plan. Members of the senior executive team participate in a planning session, which includes the following topics,

- ❖ Review interviews and evaluate results.
- ❖ Discuss the evaluated results.
- ❖ Develop short-term action plan for Fusion Management implementation.

The short-term action plan defines the following tasks necessary for a successful Fusion Management implementation.

- ❖ Personnel responsible for each task and for overall project coordination.
- ❖ A realistic schedule for completion.
- ❖ The availability of all required resources.

(1.5, 1.6) Develop Macroflowchart and Responsibility Matrix — The following interrelated steps in the process complete the first phase of the senior executive process. The senior executive team prepares flowcharts at the macro level of operations, outlining the main processes involved, including the boundaries and points of interaction between processes. From this, the group develops a detailed list of the significant functions and responsibilities of the organization. Then, executives are assigned primary and supporting roles for each responsibility.

The senior executive team has now begun the ongoing process of:

- ❖ Understanding the tools and methods of Fusion Management.
- ❖ Grasping the cultural change aspects of an undertaking of this magnitude.
- ❖ Recognizing their role in mentoring and supporting the Fusion Management process.
- ❖ Agreeing on the overall process goals.

(1.7) Analyze Business Processes — The implementation team now works with cross-functional teams to expand the macroflowchart into an overall business process map that defines in detail the subprocesses and interactions between subprocesses of the organization. The macroflowchart defines the boundaries of each subprocess and the responsibility matrix defines the process owners, key team leaders and members of the process mapping sessions. Other

team members, including staff and operational workers, are invited to participate when necessary to assure that there is a clear understanding and accurate
representation of each subprocess as it is currently being performed.

Part of the function of the business process map is to identify non-value-added
activities that can be quickly addressed. This might include eliminating unnecessary redundancies and records, reducing cycle time and improving subprocesses.

The product of this effort remains posted throughout the life of the process,
so that as changes and improvements are made, the map can be updated and
reviewed to ensure that non-value-added activities are not put back.

An important factor that differentiates Fusion Management from previous
business improvement programs is its use of documented results. In less
refined programs, results failed to drop to the bottom line due to lack of deployment or poorly defined projects. This project-by-project approach ensures
deployment of real solutions to activities that cause *real* pain. Typical average
results per project for some large organizations have been reported to be around
$200,000 to $350,000. The important feature, however, is that results are measured and process improvements are built into the management system.

STEP TWO: LAUNCH LEADERSHIP COUNCILS

In the next two activities, the organization establishes the management
structure that assures successful implementation of Fusion Management (see
Figure 6-9).

(2.1) Form Leadership Councils — In parallel with the business process
mapping activity, the senior executive team organizes the leadership council,
which will include the entire senior executive team and will be responsible for
implementing Fusion Management. The leadership council, in turn, designates

FIGURE 6-9 STEP TWO: LAUNCH LEADERSHIP COUNCILS

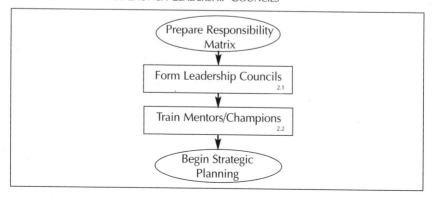

executives to serve as project mentors or champions — key management personnel who oversee, mentor and support the project teams. They become key executives in helping to select, monitor, evaluate and report on projects to the leadership council. They assure that project results are built into ongoing processes and that gains are maintained. From this group, selected executives are trained as mentors/champions. Furthermore, it is the leadership council that develops the integrated strategic plan — the plan that identifies which tactics will be deployed to achieve strategic goals.

(2.2) Train Mentors/Champions — Mentors/champions receive intensive training in Fusion Management methodology, project management and team-building techniques. The program schedule and content are tailored to the knowledge, skills and interests of the participants to maximize their learning experience. For example, workshops are based on the group's level of statistical knowledge and increase management competence. We also conduct training for leadership council members that is tailored to fit the activities they will be managing.

The mentor training program lasts anywhere from one to three weeks. The actual content will vary based on the needs of the individual members of the leadership council. Generally, the training is presented in one to three days of intensive learning followed by separate mentoring/coaching days. The one-day follow-on sessions review results, successes and lessons learned in order that midstream corrections can be made — including strengthening the knowledge base of the mentors. Mentor training includes Fusion Management concepts and management systems principles, Six Sigma methodologies and performance excellence criteria. The training describes the tools to be used, explains the cultural change aspects of an undertaking of this magnitude and defines the mentor's role in coaching and supporting individuals such as black belts and in identifying and agreeing on the overall projects and goals. These projects and goals must be integrated into the business planning process and results must be regularly reported to the leadership council.

The mentors are now prepared to participate in steps three and four, which can be carried out in parallel, since both are ongoing processes and the results of each will influence those of the other, just as the results of step five may lead to changes in steps three and four. Training in step four, for example, has to support the objectives of the strategic plan started in step three. Similarly, measures of success defined in step five have to support the objectives of the integrated strategic plan. As shown in Figure 6-6, all of the steps progress concurrently.

Step Three: Develop Integrated Strategic Plan

Utilizing the results of the baseline evaluation (1.2), responsibility matrix (1.6) and business process map (1.7), the strategic planning activities may now begin to address the as-is conditions of the management system, Lean Enterprise, Six Sigma and performance excellence. The plan, as shown in Figure 6-10, may initially address one or more of the three components in the Fusion Management hierarchy as well as any other initiatives that the enterprise may have been or still is using.

(3.1) Define Scope of Integrated Plans

Management System (Operational Level) — The overall strategic plan has to consider operational, tactical and strategic issues. The management system is the foundation for every approach that we will ultimately take. Our focus here is to ensure that we *do not "just document what we do and do what we document."* We must improve upon what we do and how we do it prior to documenting and institutionalizing our management system. If, for example, a functioning ISO 9001:2000 quality management system (or industry-specific variant) is in place, the plan may simply address how the system needs to be modified to accommodate new initiatives.

The crucial aspect of the management system process is the ongoing cycle of internal audits, preventive and corrective action and top management reviews. This is the part of the process that builds continual improvement into the organization's infrastructure. It is the feature that assures that additional tools, such as Six Sigma methodologies, will be totally integrated into the process. Building on the business process analysis developed in step one, the following items must be included in quality management systems.

- ❖ Identify system-level procedure requirements.
- ❖ Prepare or improve required system-level procedures.
- ❖ Revise quality manual.
- ❖ Prepare required work instructions.
- ❖ Train personnel and conduct internal audits.
- ❖ Perform a self-assessment audit.
- ❖ Take corrective action as needed.
- ❖ Undergo registration or compliance audit.
- ❖ Integrate into continual improvement process.

Six Sigma (Tactical Level) — Six Sigma provides the tactics that enable an enterprise to achieve breakthrough, 10x (order of magnitude) improvements. This is accomplished by training black belts to lead projects that utilize the DMAIC (Define-Measure-Analyze-Improve-Control) and DMADV (Define-Measure-Analyze-Design-Verify) processes. Since this model assumes that a quality management system is already in place, steps four and five described later emphasize Six Sigma training and implementation.

Other Initiatives (Tactical Level) — One of the most valuable aspects of Fusion Management is its use of the best features of an enterprise's prior experiences — or future desires. Processes such as Lean Enterprise, Total Quality Management and many others are brought to the table as part of the Fusion Plan. Hence, personnel selected to be groomed as facilitators, black belts, mentors, coaches, champions, etc., may be drawn from personnel previously trained in other quality initiatives — it might even be advantageous to do so.

FIGURE 6-10 STEP THREE: DEVELOP INTEGRATED STRATEGIC PLAN

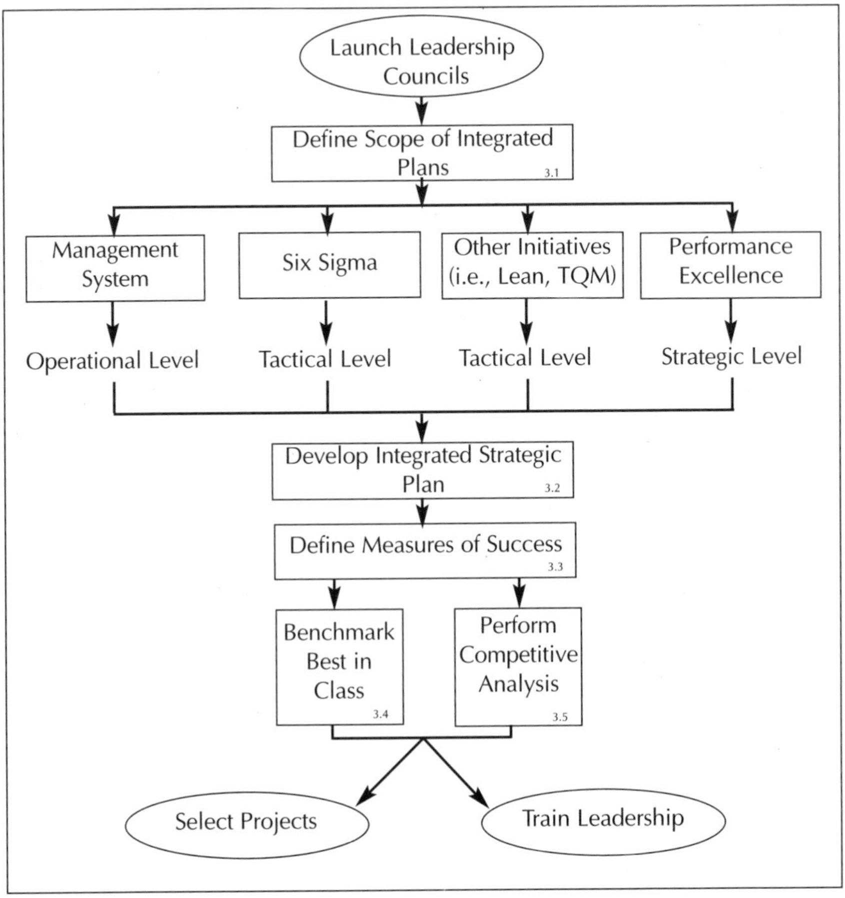

Performance Excellence (Strategic Level) — As discussed earlier in this chapter, performance excellence is the strategic component of Fusion Management. It does not prescribe how we get where we want to be, but rather provides a structure from which we can build upon any and all of the enterprise's experiences to achieve excellence. The following set of suggested activities can lead to performance excellence and can be incorporated into the strategic plan.

- ❖ Identify and train a self-assessment team.
- ❖ Perform a self-assessment using Baldrige or similar criteria.
- ❖ Analyze results of assessment.
- ❖ Prioritize opportunities for improvement.
- ❖ Prepare plan to address opportunities.
- ❖ Perform assessment of improved areas.
- ❖ Measure business results attributable to this activity.
- ❖ Continue the process.

(3.2) Develop Integrated Strategic Plan — The facilitator works closely with the leadership council to begin long-term planning. Analyses of how previous and current initiatives did or did not add value are considered. The relationship of these initiatives and their impact on Fusion Management are addressed. Planning also considers how Fusion Management can help support the cultural and business changes that an enterprise must make to move forward. Additionally, this activity includes integrating the strategic business, quality and regulatory plans, which is a unique approach for focusing managerial breakthroughs.

(3.3) Define Measures of Success — Many companies strive to be "world class." Most professionals agree, however, that defining world class is very difficult because the target is constantly moving. Some moves are incremental while others are dramatic (10x savings). With this foundation we can build a model of how we are going to get there — keeping in mind that we are chasing a moving target. This activity results in the creation and deployment of a master plan.

The measures of success are identified and shared with all associates. The dashboard created is designed to keep these key measures visible at all times. Enterprises benefit from everyone understanding the expectations, having a clear definition of how well the organization is doing and being able to rapidly respond to deviations from the optimum course.

(3.4) Benchmark Best in Class — At this point, the process is to benchmark measures of success against the competition and against the best in class, regardless of the industry. Benchmarks outside of the industry ensure that we don't fool ourselves into thinking that our industry is unique and keep us from concluding that we are achieving optimum results if we are equal to the industry's top performers. For example, a manufacturing company that wants to improve its warehousing and distribution functions may find solutions in a wide variety of noncompetitive operations.

(3.5) Perform Competitive Analysis — We have a greater opportunity than ever before to understand who our competitors are and what they are doing. Electronic networks and other information sources can expose even the most determined attempts to keep information proprietary.

STEP FOUR: TRAIN LEADERSHIP AND STAFF

Training is an ongoing process that is essential to successful Fusion Management. It may include, for example, training additional internal auditors and supplier auditors to support the management system, training personnel in new procedures, tools and methods, training in "black belt" methods to support project implementation and so forth. Here, however, as shown in Figure 6-11, we are concentrating on developing the key staff members who will lead and support implementation projects. Note that steps four and five are parts of an interrelated process: we are training leaders in step four to begin projects in step five; however, the application of these skills in carrying out projects is an essential part of their training.

(4.1) Select Pilot Projects — The mentors/champions use the information captured by the business process map, cost of nonquality, non-value-added activities, customer complaints and other sources to identify potential projects for the black belts and green belts. The training that the black belts and green belts receive will enable them to clearly define projects that will result in significant return on investment.

FIGURE 6-11 STEP FOUR: TRAIN LEADERSHIP AND STAFF

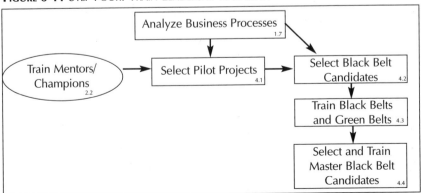

(4.2) Select Black Belt Candidates — Parallel to the selection of projects (discussed in step five) is the selection of mentors/champions. The selection is predicated on the characteristics that the senior executive team has defined as most important. The instructor/facilitator is a major resource in this activity. The role of the facilitator is to guide the senior executive team in selecting the appropriate personnel for this activity as well as guiding the mentors/champions in selecting appropriate projects.

(4.3) Train Black Belts and Green Belts — Training black belts is usually a 16-week process. Four of the 16 weeks are dedicated to classroom training, and 12 weeks are focused on using Six Sigma tools in actual projects, as described in step five. Green belts are trained as required to support particular projects or elements of projects.

(4.4) Select and Train Master Black Belt Candidates — Master black belt candidates are selected from the most proficient black belts to become the internal facilitators for Six Sigma activity. Typical selection criteria include completion of a minimum of five projects with significant results, senior executive stature, training ability, team leadership skills and quantitative analytical skills — these candidates should also be highly respected by their peers.

Step Five: Deploy the Fusion Management Process

(5.1) Deploy Fusion Management Process — The master plan defines how the Fusion Management process will be implemented and maintained throughout an enterprise — the leadership process, the review and follow-up approach, the measurement and feedback of results, the resources required and the timetable for implementation.

In earlier chapters we discussed how many programs fail due to deployment problems. We also discussed how the Baldrige process places significant weight on deployment. It is the leadership council and the senior executive process that will ensure that Fusion Management is properly deployed.

(5.2) Implement Projects — This step draws on Six Sigma tools to identify (define and measure) significant opportunities for improvement. It uses data to analyze (converts data to information), improve and control the situation to ensure that the problem does not recur. This process is generally referred to as DMAIC.

(5.3) Measure Business Results — The project's business results must be audited by the enterprise's financial department, whose function is to aid in the identification of projects that represent large opportunities for improvement.

They also must verify that the improvements are deployed and that the results can be directly seen as dropping to the bottom line.

(5.4) Implement Additional Projects — Champions, master black belts and others continue to identify areas of opportunity that are consistent with achieving the strategic goals of the enterprise.

(5.5) Measure Business Results — This becomes an ongoing responsibility of the senior executive team and represents a major change in the types of metrics that an organization identifies. It directly affects the way in which the team will construct the "dashboard" that provides visual information for better decision making.

Figure 6-12 Steps Five and Six: Deploy Fusion Management Process and Cascade Business Results

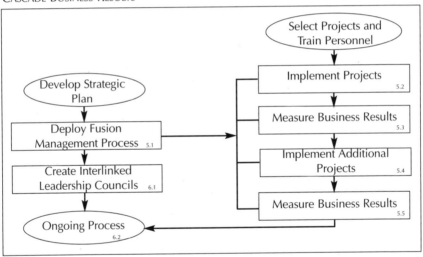

Step Six: Cascade Business Results

(6.1) Create Interlinked Leadership Councils — We recommend the creation of a cascading approach to interlinking the leadership councils in order to monitor the effective rollout of the process so that each level of leadership is represented at the next level downward and upward. This means that each facility, division, group, business unit, etc., follows a process similar to that described above, resulting in ownership at each level in the organization. Moreover, the interlinked councils assure consistency of approach and transfer of lessons learned.

Although this approach may not be necessary for a small company with one facility, it applies as soon as two facilities or divisions or product lines are involved. For larger companies, unless this approach or some alternative approach is taken, lack of an interlinking process may lead to failure of the Fusion Management endeavor.

When the process is ready to move to the next level, the senior executive team will organize their direct reports, e.g., division heads and staff functions, to form a group (business unit) leadership council that will deploy the six steps in their areas of control.

In essence, we have deployed the process throughout the organization and ensured open lines of communication. The cascade model continues to operate with each division head and functional staff member, as well as with each facility head (plant manager, research and development facility, financial center, materials center, product center) and the functional staff member cascading the process.

(6.2) Ongoing Process — The process above is replicated at each level with the integration of the implementation team, the interlinked leadership councils, the mentors, master black belts, black belts, and green belts working together to effect organizational self-sufficiency through technology and knowledge transfer. The key to the success of this (or any) process, as we have stated repeatedly, is the involvement and commitment of leadership.

LEADERSHIP DEVELOPMENT FOR FUSION MANAGEMENT

Leadership development, the key to effective Fusion Management, starts with process *cognition*, *comprehension* and *commitment* (the three Cs). This process includes:

❖ Understanding the tools and methods of Fusion Management.

❖ Grasping the cultural change aspects of an undertaking of this magnitude.

❖ Recognizing the role mentoring and support play in Fusion Management.

❖ Agreeing on the overall process goals.

This process provides the kind of in-depth understanding that the senior executive team will need to implement Fusion Management. It goes beyond commitment and ultimately results in senior executive leadership. The description that follows provides some insight into a typical intervention — to borrow a word from the social sciences. The intervention begins with organizational executives (with facilitators, wherever appropriate) discussing each other's culture, process, opportunities and barriers to success. It also establishes the vehicle and venue for creating a joint vision, plus an outline of the planning process and deployment activities required for the achievement of performance goals in the time allotted.

PHILOSOPHY OF LEADERSHIP DEVELOPMENT

The centerpiece of our philosophy is the belief that leadership (including executives from labor and management) must coach and mentor its staff. To accomplish this, leaders must first develop their own set of appropriate skills. This approach develops a leadership that enables employees to maximize their personal creative contributions toward achieving agreed-upon organizational goals. The success of the model requires managers to individually "coach" their employees. This is how an organization institutionalizes its business improvement approach. The amount of on-site training and coaching provided is customized to the specific enterprise's needs, based on:

- ❖ Type of business.
- ❖ Size of organization.
- ❖ Organizational structure.
- ❖ Corporate culture.
- ❖ National culture.
- ❖ Strategic goals and objectives.
- ❖ Current needs.
- ❖ Future wants.

We emphasize teamwork, behavior modification, change management and mentored deployment coupled with the extensive quantitative analytical skills that demonstrate breakthrough results.

EXPECTED OUTCOMES OF THE FUSION MANAGEMENT APPROACH

The senior executive team, as we have seen, participates in a process that analyzes where the company is and where it wants to be. Elements of this process include the following, which are all built into our six-step implementation model.

- ❖ Macroflowcharting the business process.
- ❖ Building a consensus responsibility matrix.

❖ Integrating strategic business, quality and regulatory plans.

❖ Benchmarking best-in-class.

❖ Recognizing and monitoring key metrics.

❖ Defining business results and needs.

❖ Mentoring next levels of management.

❖ Creating enterprise champions.

❖ Defining priority areas for project activity.

❖ Providing an environment that:

- Encourages positive change.

- Rewards risk taking.

- Develops change agents.

- Focuses on customer satisfaction.

- Is information driven.

- Emphasizes managerial breakthrough.

- Recognizes and rewards contributions of individuals and teams.

- Embraces all the stakeholders (employees, customers and suppliers) as part of the process.

STRUCTURING COACHING SESSIONS FOR SENIOR MANAGEMENT

In order to keep the senior executive team and the cascading levels of management aware of and committed to Fusion Management, we recommend holding an ongoing series of structured coaching sessions, with such a series built into the implementation process.

❖ *The target audience starts with the senior executive team and then cascades through the organization*, eventually touching every manager. In parallel, all employees are involved in the improvement of their processes.

❖ *Contents of sessions vary.* The senior executive team will most likely participate in a number of prescribed interventions over the first few months, setting the foundation for Fusion Management and supporting the enterprise's emphasis on customer satisfaction.

❖ *Regular (monthly) meetings of the senior executive team are held, perhaps using a third-party facilitator (at least in the beginning) to coach the deployment of the evolving process and to confront any barriers encountered.* Similar start-up activities and ongoing monthly management reviews will take place throughout the enterprise (the facilities, service centers, operating centers, etc.).

The aim of this effort is to bring each management team to self-sufficiency through knowledge/technology transfer. Built into this model is a process whereby the facilitator initiates early interventions and then enlists personnel to serve as master black belts in training. When these master black belts are qualified, they will be able to perform many duties with the senior executive team as knowledge/technology transfer agents.

Developing an Evaluation Checklist for Fusion Management

As part of this discipline, the Fusion Management approach creates metrics to gauge the effectiveness of the business process and its impact on business results. Projects are evaluated against the baseline data and postproject deployment results. The project evaluation checklist focuses on results in such areas as:

❖ Business process improvement.

❖ Design and design control.

❖ Process variation/validation.

❖ Customer focus/approach.

❖ Change management.

❖ Self-assessment.

❖ Registered management systems.

❖ 10x improvement.

❖ Cycle time reduction.

Conclusion: The Never-Ending Process

The ongoing process of continual improvement demands continual monitoring to ensure that the organization does not regress — hence, the senior executive process and the cascading leadership councils. Changes of personnel at any level in the organization can deliberately or unwittingly erode the gains that the organization has worked to attain.

Bringing in new executives and key staff members creates a constant challenge to any organization. The newcomer feels compelled to place his or her brand on what the enterprise is doing and the way in which it is doing it. Moreover, the purpose of Fusion Management is to encourage healthy and constructive change. Thus, the management system and the change process implemented must be robust enough to allow new executives to bring their prior experiences to the enterprise and seamlessly "fuse" them to that which is already in place. Successful enterprises are designed to be able to assimilate new ideas and new methods. That is how they are able to continue to grow effectively and efficiently. The Fusion Management process must address the need for both continual improvement and breakthrough innovation — and view them both as integral parts of the never-ending journey towards excellence.

Acronyms

AEC	Atomic Energy Commission
AIAG	Automotive Industry Action Group
ANSI	American National Standards Institute
AQAP	Allied Quality Assurance Publication
AQL	Acceptable Quality Level
AS	Aerospace Standards
ASME	American Society of Mechanical Engineers
ASQ	American Society for Quality
ASQC	American Society for Quality Control (now ASQ)
BSI	British Standards Institution
CASE	Coordinated Aerospace Supplier Evaluation
CE	Conformite Europeene
CEO	Chief Executive Officer
COQ	Cost Of Quality
CFR	US Code of Federal Regulations
CPSC	Consumer Product Safety Commission
CQI	Continuous Quality Improvement
DFSS	Design For Six Sigma
DMAIC	Define-Measure-Analyze-Improve-Control

DMADV	Define-Measure-Analyze-Design-Verify
DoD	US Department of Defense
DoE	US Department of Energy
DOE	Design Of Experiments
DPMO	Defects Per Million Opportunities
DPU	Defects Per Unit
DTD	Dock To Dock
ECN	Engineering Change Notice
EFQM	European Foundation for Quality Management
EOQ	European Organization for Quality
EPA	US Environmental Protection Agency
EQA	European Quality Award
EU	European Union
FAA	Federal Aviation Administration
FAR	Federal Acquisition Regulation
FBM	Fleet Ballistic Missile
FCC	Federal Communications Commission
FDA	US Food and Drug Administration
FLSA	Fair Labor Standards Act
FMEA	Failure Mode and Effects Analysis
FPS	Ford Production System
GE	General Electric
GMP	Good Manufacturing Practice
HSPD	Handling, Storage, Packaging and Delivery
IAEA	International Atomic Energy Agency
IBM	International Business Machines
IQA	Institute of Quality Assurance (UK)
IQF	International Quality Federation
IRS	Internal Revenue Service
ISO	International Organization for Standardization
JIT	Just-In-Time
JUSE	Japanese Union of Scientists and Engineers
LTPD	Lot Tolerance Percent Defective

MBO	Management by Objectives
MBNQA	Malcolm Baldrige National Quality Award
MITI	Ministry of International Trade and Industry
NASA	National Aeronautics and Space Administration
NATO	North Atlantic Treaty Organization
NBC	National Broadcasting Company
NDIA	National Defense Industrial Association
NHK	Japanese Broadcasting Company
NIST	National Institute for Standards and Technology
NRC	US Nuclear Regulatory Commission
OCC	Operating Characteristic Curve
OEE	Overall Equipment Effectiveness
OHIP	Office of Health and Industry Programs
OSHA	Occupational Safety and Health Agency
OSMA	Office of Small Manufacturers Assistance
PDA	Personal Digital Assistant
PDC	Product Development Cycle
PDSA	Plan-Do-Study-Act
P&L	Profit and Loss
P&S	Products and Services
QA	Quality Analysis
QC	Quality Control
QCRG	Quality Control Research Group
QFD	Quality Function Deployment
QNJ	Quality New Jersey
QSR	Quality System Regulation
QuEST	Quality Excellence for Suppliers of Telecommunications
RCA	Radio Corporation of America
R&D	Research & Development
ROI	Return On Investment
SAE	Society of Automotive Engineers
SAM	STAT-A-MATRIX, Inc.
SBP	Strategic Business Plan

SEC	US Securities and Exchange Commission
SET	Senior Executive Team
SME	Small and Medium Enterprises
SMED	Single-Minute Exchange of Die
SPC	Statistical Process Control
SQC	Statistical Quality Control
SQP	Strategic Quality Plan
SRP	Strategic Regulatory Plan
SUV	Sports Utility Vehicle
SWOT	Strengths, Weaknesses, Opportunities and Threats
TPM	Total Productive Maintenance
TPS	Toyota Production System
TQM	Total Quality Management
VDA	Verband der Automobilindustrie (Germany)
VOC	Voice of the Customer
ZD	Zero Defects

Bibliography

21 CFR Part 820, Good Manufacturing Practice for Medical Devices. Washington: Food and Drug Administration, US Code of Federal Regulations, Federal Register, 1978.

1998 AlliedSignal Annual Report. Morristown: AlliedSignal Inc. Corporate Publications, 1998.

1998 General Electric Annual Report. Fairfield: General Electric Company, 1999.

1999 American Express Annual Report. New York: American Express Company, 1999.

1999 General Electric Annual Report. Fairfield: General Electric Company, 2000.

1999 Honeywell Annual Report. Morristown: Honeywell International Inc. Corporate Publications, 1999.

1999 Kodak Annual Report. Rochester: Eastman Kodak Company, 1999.

2000 General Electric Annual Report. Fairfield: General Electric Company, 2001.

Albrecht, Karl. *Successful Management by Objectives — An Action Manual.* Englewood Cliffs: Prentice-Hall, 1978.

ANSI N45.2 Daughter Documents, American National Standards Institute Quality Assurance Program Requirements for Nuclear Power Plants. New York: American Society of Mechanical Engineers, 1971.

ANSI/ASME NQA-1, Quality Assurance Program Requirements for Nuclear Facilities. New York: American Society of Mechanical Engineers, 1989.

ANSI/ASME N45.2, American National Standards Institute Quality Assurance Program Requirements for Nuclear Power Plants. New York: American Society of Mechanical Engineers, 1971.

ANSI/ASME NA4000, ASME Boiler and Pressure Vessel Code, Section iii, Division I, Subsection NA, Rules for Construction of Nuclear Power Plant Components, Quality Assurance. New York: American Society of Mechanical Engineers, 1971.

AS9100, Quality Management Systems – Aerospace. Warrendale: Society of Automotive Engineers, 1999.

BS5750, Quality Systems. London: British Standards Institution, 1979.

Byrne, John A. "Strategic Planning." *Business Week* 26 August 1996.

Canadian National Standard Z299: Guide for Selecting and Implementing the CAN3-Z299-85 Quality Assurance Program Standards. Toronto: Canadian Standards Association, 1997.

CE Marking, Directive 98/34/EC. Brussels: European Commission, 1999.

Crosby, Philip. *Zero Defects: Myth and Reality.* Winter Park: Phil Crosby and Associates, 2001.

Deming, W. Edwards. *Elementary Principles of the Statistical Control of Quality.* Tokyo: Nippon Kagaku Gijutsu Renmei, 1950.

The Deming Prize. Tokyo: Union of Japanese Scientists & Engineers (JUSE), 2001.

Dickson, W.J., and F.D. Roethlisberger. *Management and the Worker.* Cambridge: Harvard UP, 1939.

Dodge, Harold French, and Harry G. Romig. *Sampling Inspection Tables: Single and Double Sampling, 2nd Revised and Expanded Edition.* New York: John Wiley & Sons, 1959.

European Quality Award. Brussels: European Foundation for Quality Management, 2001.

Feigenbaum, Armand V. *Total Quality Control.* New York: McGraw-Hill, 1961.

George, Neil. "Ratings Full of Hot Air." *Inside Webster* 16 October 2001.

Gimpel, Jean. *The Medieval Machine.* New York: Holt, Rinehart and Winston, 1976.

Governor's Award for Performance Excellence. Trenton: Quality New Jersey, 2000.

Hammer, Michael, and James Champy. *Reengineering the Corporation: A Manifesto for Business Revolution*. New York: Harper Collins Publishers, 1993.

Healey, James R. "January memo revealed tire flaws Firestone execs linked cost of defects, Decatur." Arlington: *USA Today* 8 September 2000.

Imai, Masaaki. *Kaizen: The Key to Japan's Competitive Success*. New York: McGraw-Hill, 1986.

Ishikawa, Kaoru. *What is Total Quality Control? The Japanese Way*. Englewood Cliffs: Prentice-Hall, 1985.

ISO 9000 Registered Company Directory North America. Vol 5. No. 4. CD-ROM. Fairfax: QSU Publishing Company, 2002.

ISO 9001:1994: Quality Systems — Model for Quality Assurance in Design, Production, Installation and Servicing. Geneva: International Organization for Standardization, 1994.

ISO 9001:2000: Quality Management Systems – Requirements. Geneva: International Organization for Standardization, 2000.

ISO 10011, Guidelines for Auditing Quality Systems — Qualification Criteria for Quality Systems Auditors. Geneva: International Organization for Standardization, 1991.

ISO 14001:1996: Environmental Management Systems — Specifications with Guide. Geneva: International Organization for Standardization, 1996.

ISO/TS 16949, Quality Systems — Automotive Suppliers — Particular Requirements for the Application of ISO 9001:1994. Geneva: International Automotive Task Force, International Organization for Standardization, 1999.

Jones, Del. "Quality Auditor OK'd Decatur Tire Plant." *USA Today* 8 September 2000.

Juran, J.M. *Managerial Breakthrough*. New York: McGraw-Hill, 1964.

Malcolm Baldrige National Quality Award, 1990. Gaithersburg: US Department of Commerce, Technology Administration, National Institute of Standards and Technology, 1990.

Malcolm Baldrige National Quality Award, 1988 Application Guidelines. Gaithersburg: US Department of Commerce, Technology Administration, National Institute of Standards and Technology, 1988.

Malcolm Baldrige National Quality Award, 2001 Application Guidelines. Gaithersburg: US Department of Commerce, Technology Administration, National Institute of Standards and Technology, 2001.

McGregor, Douglas. *Leadership and Motivation*. Cambridge: M.I.T. Press, 1966.

Merriam-Webster's Collegiate Dictionary, 10th ed. Springfield: Merriam-Webster, 2001.

MIL-Q-21549, Product Quality Program Requirements for Fleet Balistic Missile Weapon System Contractors. Washington: US Government Printing Office, 1963.

MIL-Q-9858A, Military Specification: Quality Program Requirements. Washington: US Government Printing Office, 1959.

MIL-STD-105. Sampling Procedures and Tables for Inspection by Attributes. Washington: US Government Printing Office, 1963.

MIL-STD-414. Sampling Procedures and Table for Inspection by Variables for Percent Defective. Washington: US Government Printing Office, 1957.

NASA Quality Publication NPC 200-2, Quality Programs for Space System Contractors. Washington: Government Printing Office, 1962.

NATO Requirements for an Industrial Quality Control System. Washington: Allied Quality Assurance Publication, 1968.

Nordstrom, Elmer. *A Winning Team*. Seattle: Elmer Nordstrom, 1985.

NRC 10-CFR 50, Appendix B, Part 10: Energy, Quality Assurance Criteria for Nuclear Power Plants and Fuel Reprocessing Plants. Washington: Government Printing Office, 1970.

Obaba, Al-Iman. *The Papyrus Ebers: Oldest Medical Book in the World*. New York: African Islamic Mission Publications, 1927.

OHSAS 18001: Occupational Health and Safety Management Systems Specifications. London: British Standards Institution, 1999.

Osada, Takashi. *The 5 S's: Five Keys to a Total Quality Environment*. Portland: Productivity, 1991.

Ouchi, William G. *Theory Z: How American Business Can Meet the Japanese Challenge*. Reading: Addison-Wesley, 1981.

President's Quality Award Program. Washington: US Office of Executive and Management Development, Personnel Management, 2001.

Reagan, Ronald. "State of the Union Address." Washington: Library of Congress, 1987.

Rosander, A.C. *Applications of Quality Control to the Service Industry*. New York: Marcel Dekker, 1985.

Sheaffer, C.R. "What Top Management Expects from Quality Control." First Annual Convention American Society for Quality Control. Chicago, 5 June 1947.

SA8000: Social Accountability. New York: Social Accountability International, 2001.

Shewhart, W.A. *Economic Control of Quality of Manufactured Product.* New York: D. Van Nostrand Company, 1931.

Smith, Adam. *An Inquiry into the Nature and Causes of the Wealth of Nations.* London: Methuen and Company, 1776.

Taylor, Frederick Winslow. *The Principles of Scientific Management.* New York: Harper Brothers, 1911.

A Text on Quality Control for Foremen. Tokyo: JUSE, 1957.

TL 9000, Quality Management System Requirements Handbook 1, Release 3.0. Milwaukee: QuEST Forum, Quality Press, 2001.

US Consumer Product Safety Commission, Handbook and Standard for Manufacturing Safer Consumer Products. Washington: Office of Information and Public Affairs, 1975.

Walton, Mary. *The Deming Management Method.* New York: Putnam Publishing Group, 1986.

White, Joseph B. "Next Big Thing — Reengineering Gurus Take Steps to Remodel Their Stalling Vehicles." *Wall Street Journal* 26 November 1996.

Authors

STANLEY A. MARASH

Stanley A. Marash is chairman and CEO of The SAM Group, which includes STAT-A-MATRIX and Oriel Incorporated. Marash consults and lectures throughout the world to heads of state and corporations on regulatory and compliance processes, Six Sigma and the integration of quality, regulatory and business management systems — an approach that led to development of his Fusion Management concept. He is the author of articles on quality management systems and business process improvement, and for many years has touted the synthesis of the qualitative and quantitative aspects of management processes. He holds a Ph.D. in management and M.B.A. and baccalaureate degrees in applied statistics. He is a certified quality engineer and a certified reliability engineer; chairman emeritus and founder of Quality New Jersey; a former Baldrige examiner; founder and past chairman of the World Quality Council; a fellow of the American Society for Quality; and a recipient of the Ellis R. Ott Award and the E.J. Lancaster Medal. For more information about STAT-A-MATRIX, visit http://www.statamatrix.com.

PAUL BERMAN

Paul Berman, vice president, STAT-A-MATRIX, has spent more than 12 years at STAT-A-MATRIX preparing and presenting materials on quality management systems. Previously, he spent over 30 years in the aerospace and defense industries. As director of product support for Lockheed Electronics, a division of Lockheed-Martin, he managed worldwide support planning, technical documentation, customer training, spare parts, repair and overhaul, field services, reliability and maintainability and logistics support functions. He holds B.A. and M.A. degrees and served in the US Army as a radar technician. He taught business and technical communications part time at Rutgers University for 16 years and has authored many articles on ISO 9000, management systems, product reliability, technical documentation and product support.

MICHAEL F. FLYNN

Michael F. Flynn, executive director, consulting services, STAT-A-MATRIX, has successfully applied modern management techniques to continuous improvement of business processes. For STAT-A-MATRIX he currently teaches and consults in Six Sigma and related methodologies. Most recently, he was instrumental in designing a quality management system training program for a major international agency. He has more than 20 years of experience in the metal, food, packaging, chemical and pharmaceutical industries. His expertise includes course design and delivery, Six Sigma, TQM, ISO 9000, SPC, process mapping, cycle time reduction, experimental design, system documentation and reliability. He holds M.S. and B.A. degrees in mathematics and is a certified quality engineer. He is also a widely published science-fiction author.

Index